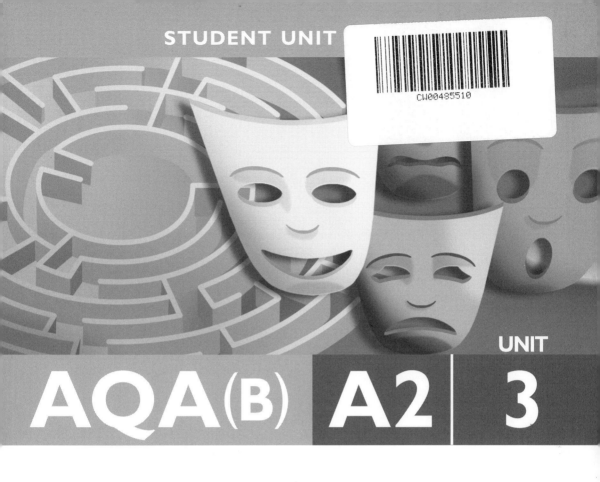

STUDENT UNIT

AQA(B) A2

UNIT

3

Psychology

Child Development and Applied Options

Julie McLoughlin

Philip Allan Updates, an imprint of Hodder Education, an Hachette UK company, Market Place, Deddington, Oxfordshire OX15 0SE

Orders

Bookpoint Ltd, 130 Milton Park, Abingdon, Oxfordshire OX14 4SB
tel: 01235 827720
fax: 01235 400454
e-mail: uk.orders@bookpoint.co.uk

Lines are open 9.00 a.m.–5.00 p.m., Monday to Saturday, with a 24-hour message answering service. You can also order through the Philip Allan Updates website: www.philipallan.co.uk

© Philip Allan Updates 2009

ISBN 978-0-340-95955-8

First printed 2009
Impression number 5 4 3 2
Year 2014 2013 2012 2011 2010

This guide has been written specifically to support students preparing for the AQA Specification B A2 Psychology Unit 3 examination. The content has been neither approved nor endorsed by AQA and remains the sole responsibility of the author.

Typeset by Pantek Arts Ltd, Maidstone
Printed by MPG Books, Bodmin

Hachette UK's policy is to use papers that are natural, renewable and recyclable products and made from wood grown in sustainable forests. The logging and manufacturing processes are expected to conform to the environmental regulations of the country of origin.

Contents

Introduction

■ ■ ■

Content Guidance

■ ■ ■

Questions and Answers

Introduction

About this guide

This is a guide to Unit 3 of the AQA(B) A2 psychology specification. The guide is intended as a revision aid rather than as a textbook. The purpose of the guide is to summarise the content, to explain how the content will be assessed, to look at the type of questions to expect, and to consider specimen answers.

There are eight topic areas in Unit 3 and you have to answer questions on three of these topics in your examination. You must answer one question from the child development section and two from the applied options section. The choice of topics is shown in Table 1.

Table 1 Choice of topics

Child development (choose one topic)	Applied options (choose two topics)
Social development	Cognition and law
Cognitive development	Schizophrenia and mood disorders
Moral development	Stress and stress management
	Substance abuse
	Forensic psychology

For each of these topics, this guide will cover the following:
- the specification content, which tells you exactly what you need to know and learn
- appropriate content relevant to the topic. This gives you minimal coverage of the topic, as you should already have covered the details in your studies. The focus is on key terms and concepts, key theories and studies and evaluation points. The content here is not the only appropriate material; textbooks will cover the topics in various ways and probably give much more detail as well as alternative studies.
- a sample question in the style of AQA(B) A2 questions, similar to those that you might expect to see on real examination papers
- an analysis of how the question should be tackled and what the examiners are looking for in an answer
- a typical grade-C/D student answer (candidate A), together with examiner comments showing where the marks have been gained and lost, drawing attention to any errors and giving suggestions as to how the answers might be improved or elaborated to get extra marks
- a typical grade-A student answer (candidate B), followed by examiner comments that show which points are especially creditworthy.

If you read these sample answers and comments carefully, you will learn a lot about what you need to do to present a really effective answer in the examination.

How to use this guide

First, check your class notes and revision notes against the content presented here to make sure that you have all the right material for your revision. Then look at a sample question to see how the examination is structured and what is required. Try to answer the question, and then examine the sample answers and comments to see where credit can be gained and lost. The sample answers are not intended as model answers but as tools to help you understand what makes a good answer. Finally, you should review your own answer in light of what you have read and consider how your own response to the question might be improved.

The examination

The Unit 3 examination is 2 hours long and you have to answer three questions: one on child development and two on applied options. Each question carries 20 marks, so you should allow 40 minutes for each question in the examination.

All questions are structured, which means that there are several sub-sections to each question. The first sub-sections are usually short-answer questions worth 1, 2, 3 or 4 marks. These are followed by a final sub-section that requires extended writing for 12 marks.

Short-answer questions
- Commands such as 'identify', 'state', 'name' 'suggest' and 'give' require only the briefest of answers.
- Questions that contain commands such as 'outline' and 'describe' require straight-forward descriptions.
- Verbs such as 'explain' and 'distinguish' indicate that some analysis or elaboration of concepts is required. In the case of 'distinguish', you need to explain the difference(s) between two concepts.
- The command 'briefly discuss' requires some description and some evaluation or criticism, and is usually worth 4 or 5 marks.
- If asked to 'describe a study' for 4 marks, you should refer explicitly to the aim, method, results and conclusion of the study.

Examples of short-answer questions
- Identify **two** stages of moral reasoning proposed by Kohlberg.
- Explain what is meant by *labelling* in relation to schizophrenia.
- Give **two** consequences of rejection.
- State what is meant by *false memory*.
- Outline what psychologists mean by *conservation*.
- Describe **one** study in which eyewitness identification procedures were investigated.
- Briefly discuss **one** limitation of behaviour modification as a treatment for offending.
- Distinguish between problem-focused and emotion-focused strategies for stress management.

Long-answer questions

These are worth 12 marks. A typical 12-mark question would ask you to 'describe and evaluate' a theory, an explanation or some research. In 12-mark questions, there are 4 marks for description and knowledge and 8 marks for evaluation/ analysis/application. In the evaluation, you should present strengths and limitations. If relevant, you should support what you say with reference to evidence and explain how the evidence relates to the topic. You can also get evaluation marks by comparing — for example, introducing an opposing theory to illustrate the limitations of the theory you are discussing. You should aim to spend plenty of time on this sub-section of the question in the examination.

In the 12-mark questions you will be assessed on your ability to communicate. You should therefore make sure that your answer is properly structured into sentences and paragraphs, and pay attention to your spelling. If a 12-mark question asks you to 'refer to evidence' or 'refer to an alternative explanation', there will be a limit to the number of marks that you will be awarded if you do not comply with that instruction.

Mark schemes for 12-mark questions are banded into 'excellent', 'good to average', 'average to poor' and 'poor' bands. This means that the examiner will not only consider each individual point that you make, but will also make a global assessment of the answer as a whole. Candidates who show extensive knowledge and make lots of evaluation points but who do not present a well-argued response will sometimes be awarded a lower mark than they might have been given. This is because the answer as a whole is better suited to the 'good to average' band than the 'excellent' band.

Scenario questions

In some questions, you must use your knowledge by applying what you have learned about psychology to a novel situation. For example, a question might include a scenario about two people who show different responses to a stressful situation. In this case, you might be required to use your knowledge of stress to explain the experiences or behaviours of the people in the scenario. For example, you could describe how people with certain types of personality seem to cope with stress better than other personality types. This sort of question tests the application of knowledge.

Assessment of practical psychology and research methods

In Unit 3, your knowledge of practical psychology and research methods will be tested in the context of the child development questions. For example, there may be a cognitive development question in which you are asked about a study of cognitive development that has been described to you. In this unit, questions on research methods and practical psychology will be restricted to the content of research methods in Unit 1 and what you have covered through your own practical exercises in class. You will not be expected to know about inferential statistics, statistical tests or the issues in the research section of Unit 4.

It is therefore important that you re-read and revise the research methods section of Unit 1 before you take the Unit 3 examination.

Content
Guidance

In this section, content guidance is offered on the topic areas of child development and applied options. Each topic begins with a summary of the AQA Specification B requirements for Unit 3. This is followed by a brief account of the theories and studies that make up the unit content.

Knowledge of appropriate theories and studies is essential for the A2 examination. It is also important to be able to assess their value, and this is done here with regular 'Evaluation' features that provide criticisms of both.

Names and publication dates have been given when referring to research studies. The full details for these studies are normally available in textbooks, should you wish to research the topic further.

Child development
Social development

Early relationships

Summary specification content

Attachment and the role of caregiver–infant interactions in the development of attachment, including reference to human and animal studies. Function of attachment. Secure and insecure attachments. Measuring attachment.

Possible short-term and long-term consequences of privation and deprivation.

Romanian orphan studies: effects of institutionalisation, age-related benefits of adoption (Rutter et al.).

The work of Bowlby, Schaffer, Ainsworth and van Ijzendoorn.

The role of caregiver–infant interactions

Various aspects of caregiver–infant interactions help to develop and maintain attachment. These include imitation, interactional synchrony, physical contact, modified language and sensitive responsiveness.

Imitation

Melzoff and Moore (1977) found that 2- to 3-week-old babies would imitate adults' facial expressions and movements. They concluded that even tiny babies will spontaneously imitate face and hand movements.

Interactional synchrony

Condon and Sander (1974) analysed babies' movements when an adult was speaking to them. They found that babies would move in time with the conversation and 'take turns' — reciprocal behaviour. Isabella et al. (1989) found more interactional synchrony in securely attached mother–baby pairs.

Physical contact

Klaus and Kennell (1976) suggested that immediate contact and skin-to-skin stimulation in the period after birth was important for the formation of a bond.

Modified language (motherese)

Motherese is a slow, high-pitched, repetitive way of speaking to young babies that involves short, simple sentences and varying tone. It aids communication and may contribute to effective turn-taking, aiding attachment.

Sensitive responsiveness

Ainsworth (1978) found that the type and quality of attachment depended on the behaviour of the mother (see Ainsworth's strange situation on p. 11).

- Imitation may not be intentional communication.

- Cross-cultural work suggests interactional synchrony is not linked to attachment (LeVine et al., 1994).

- Immediate physical contact is not essential for attachment.

- Adults use motherese with all babies and young children. There is no direct evidence that it affects attachment.

- Cross-cultural evidence suggests that sensitive responsiveness is not always necessary for secure attachment.

Animal research

Studies with monkeys suggest that infant–caregiver interaction is important for the development of attachment.

Study: Harlow (1959)

Harlow studied infant rhesus monkeys separated from their mothers at birth. The caged infants had two substitute mothers: a soft cloth mother and a wire mother with a feeding bottle. The infants spent more time with the cloth mother, visiting the wire mother just for food. When later introduced to normal monkeys, the separated infants showed delinquent behaviour; they were aggressive and unable to form relationships. Harlow concluded that attachment depends on physical comfort more than on food and that a lack of attachment leads to antisocial behaviour.

Evaluation

- Harlow's research caused distress to the infant monkeys.

- It may be inappropriate to generalise from monkeys to human attachment.

Function of attachment

- **Cupboard-love theory** — babies attach to those who feed them. Harlow's study suggests this is incorrect.
- **Survival theory** — according to evolutionary theory, attachment aids survival. Observations show how young animals often attach instinctively to the first large moving object they see (**imprinting**) (Lorenz, 1935). Psychoanalytic theorists (e.g. Bowlby, 1969) proposed that human infants have an **innate, instinctual drive** to keep proximity to the caregiver.
- **Communication theory** — Bower (1979) suggested that infants choose to attach to the person with whom they can best communicate; the person who is most sensitive to the child's communication. This explanation links to Ainsworth's views about sensitive responsiveness.
- **The internal working model** — Bowlby (1969) proposed that a child's earliest attachment provides an internal working model of relationships, which is used as a framework for future relationships. Dunn (1993) argued that the concept is too general to be useful.

Measuring attachment: secure and insecure attachments

We shall consider three methods: the strange situation (observational method), the adult attachment interview (interview method) and the attachment Q-sort (psychological test).

The strange situation (Ainsworth)

Ainsworth et al. (1978) carried out a controlled observation of brief separations from the mother. In a series of 3-minute episodes, infant and mother were observed with the researcher, the researcher left the room, a stranger entered, the mother left, the mother returned etc. Behaviours such as proximity seeking and maintenance of proximity were recorded. Infants were classified as securely attached (65%), anxious avoidant or anxious resistant (15–20% each). Ainsworth concluded that there are different types of attachments and the type depends on the mother's sensitivity and responsiveness.

Evaluation

- Category percentages are similar in many cultures.

- Proximity seeking may not be a valid measure. Secure infants do not always stay close to the mother and are happy to explore (Cassidy, 1986).

- Ainsworth neglected temperament, family background etc.

- Fraley and Spieker (2003) suggested two dimensions to attachment: proximity seeking versus avoidance, and anger/resistance versus emotional confidence.

The strange situation (van Ijzendoorn)

Van Ijzendoorn and Kroonenberg (1988) compared 32 strange situation studies from eight countries. They found more anxious-avoidant attachments in Germany and more anxious-resistant attachments in Israel and Japan. This suggests different child-rearing practices affect the type of attachment. De Wolff and van Ijzendoorn (1997) found only a weak link between the mother's sensitivity and security of attachment.

The adult attachment interview (Main et al., 1985)

The adult attachment interview is a 1-hour interview with 15 open questions about attachment experience. Responses are categorised as insecure-dismissing, autonomous-secure, insecure-preoccupied or unresolved. Autonomous-secure individuals discuss their own experiences openly and have securely attached children.

The attachment Q-sort

This test involves sorting a set of 90 cards into piles according to how true the card description is of the child's behaviour. An attachment score is then calculated.

Consequences of privation and deprivation

Privation is never having had a secure and loving relationship with an attachment figure. Animal research (e.g. Harlow's monkey study on p. 10) showed that privated monkeys became delinquent and aggressive. Case studies of severely neglected individuals provide evidence for the effects of privation on humans. Genie (Curtiss, 1977) was neglected until the age of 13 years. She was physically underdeveloped and had no language skills. Although her condition improved when taken into care, she never really recovered from her years of privation. In other cases, people have overcome the effects of privation.

> ### Study: Koluchova (1991)
> Koluchova studied twin boys who had been locked in a cellar from the age of 18 months old. At 7 years they went into care and were later fostered. By 10 years their IQ level was average. They had normal family attachments. As adults, they had jobs and families. The years of privation seem to have been overcome.

Deprivation is having a secure relationship with an attachment figure and then losing it. **Short-term consequences** of deprivation include a sequence of behaviour known as **protest–despair–detachment**. This was shown by Robertson and Robertson (1968), who filmed the distress of young children going into care. Schaffer (1996) suggested that boys suffer most in separations. Other factors are a difficult temperament, previous family conflict and repeat separations. **Long-term consequences** of deprivation include separation anxiety — fear of being abandoned by an attachment figure resulting in increased clinginess and stress symptoms. For adults, separation anxiety may cause insecurity in relationships and lack of trust. Some studies show that children of divorced parents (who often experience separation) have lower academic attainment and higher rates of delinquency. However, this could be due to other problems such as a general disruption of lifestyle.

> ### Study: Belsky (1988)
> Belsky analysed the combined results of several studies into the effects of daycare on attachment. The results suggested that attachment is negatively affected if a child spends more than 20 hours a week in non-maternal care.

Romanian orphan studies and the effects of institutionalisation
Large numbers of Romanian children were found to be suffering extreme privation in orphanages in the 1990s. Many were adopted in the UK and they have been studied by the English and Romanian Adoptees (ERA) study team.

Age-related benefits of adoption
Rutter et al. (1998) compared Romanian orphans adopted in the UK with a control group of British adopted children. Four years after adoption there were no significant differences between the two groups in physical and cognitive development. However, the greatest 'catch-up' was seen in those who had arrived in Britain before 6 months of age.

Other ERA findings indicate that the consequences for children adopted after 6 months are not so positive. The Romanian institution-reared adoptees showed more autistic-like symptoms and unusual attachment behaviours than the UK controls. Beckett et al. (2006) found that many Romanian children aged over 6 months at the time of adoption continued to show negative cognitive effects at 11 years.

Evaluation

- Rutter's original view that the effects of privation can be overcome may be over-optimistic. For adoption after 6 months, the consequences seem long-lasting.

- The ERA research is large scale and well controlled. Previous work involved single cases or animal experiments.

- Negative effects may not be due to institutionalisation alone, but due to a severely impoverished and unstimulating environment.

Bowlby's theory of attachment

Bowlby stated that mother love in infancy is just as important for a child's mental health as are vitamins and minerals for physical health. He suggested that young children need 'a warm, intimate and continuous relationship with mother'.

Main points

- Infants have an **innate** need to attach to one figure — **monotropy**.
- Young children need the continuous care of this person for the first 2 years — a **critical period**.
- Breaking of the attachment bond in the critical period results in **irreversible** long-term damage to the child.
- The **consequences** of maternal deprivation include delinquency, affectionless behaviour and intellectual retardation.

Evidence

- Harlow's monkey study (see p. 10) supported the view that separation from the mother had long-term consequences.
- Lorenz's research with geese showed that attachment behaviour (following behaviour) is innate in other species.
- Goldfarb (1943) compared outcomes for children raised in an institution and children who had been fostered. The group that had spent 3 years in an institution scored less well on cognitive and emotional tests.
- Bowlby carried out retrospective interviews with 44 juvenile thieves, 14 of whom were described as affectionless psychopaths who showed no feelings for others. Bowlby found that most of the affectionless individuals were separated from their mother in the first 2 years. Bowlby concluded that maternal deprivation in childhood leads to delinquency and affectionless behaviour.

Evaluation

- Bowlby confused deprivation and privation.
- Delinquency is related to the causes and circumstances of separation (e.g. family trauma) and how the separation is handled (Rutter, 1981).

- Hodges and Tizard (1989) argued against the 2-year critical period. They showed that children adopted at 7 years could develop attachments.

- Some animal studies suggest that the effects of early deprivation are reversible (Suomi and Harlow, 1972).

- Freud and Dann (1951) found that effective substitute care could mediate the effects of early separation. ERA research suggests that 'catch-up' is possible if adoption occurs early enough.

- Schaffer and Emerson (1964) argued against monotropy. Their study of Scottish infants showed that multiple attachments are the norm.

The work of Schaffer

Schaffer and Emerson (1964) studied attachment in 60 Glaswegian infants. They proposed four stages of attachment development:
- **(1)** the **asocial** stage (0–6 weeks) — babies do not differentiate much between people and objects
- **(2)** the **diffuse** stage (6 weeks–6 months) — babies have no obviously preferred attachment figure
- **(3)** the **single attachment** stage (7–12 months) — babies show a strong preference for one attachment figure with fear of strangers
- **(4)** the **multiple attachment** stage (over 12 months) — most children have up to five attachment figures by 18 months

Later relationships

Summary specification content

The development of friendship in childhood and adolescence. Age-related change in friendship. Sex differences in children's friendship.

Research into the causes and consequences of popularity and rejection.

Friendship in childhood and adolescence

According to Smith et al. (2003) friendship is 'a close relationship between two particular people, as indicated by their association together or their psychological attachment and trust'.

Age-related change in friendship

Most research focuses on changes in the understanding of friendship with age. Selman (1980) suggested **five stages** of friendship understanding:
- **(1)** 3–6 years — physical partner
- **(2)** 5–9 years — one-way assistant
- **(3)** 7–12 years — reciprocity
- **(4)** 10–15 years — exclusive intimacy
- **(5)** over 12 years — autonomous interdependence

Study: Damon (1977)

Damon asked children questions about friendship. Under the age of 7 years, friendship is about who you play with. At 8–11 years, friendship is about shared interests, trust and kindness. From 12 years, friendship is about mutual understanding and intimacy. Damon concluded that understanding of friendship changes with age as children become less egocentric.

Study: Bigelow and La Gaipa (1975)

Bigelow and La Gaipa studied children's 'my best friend' stories. Younger children's stories focused on living close, play and common interests, whereas older children referred more to loyalty and intimacy. The researchers concluded that as children get older, there is less emphasis on physical interaction and more focus on psychological characteristics and concern for others.

Evaluation

- Language ability may be a confounding variable in some studies. Older children can express complex emotional ideas more easily than younger children.

- Categorisation of dilemma responses/content of stories may be subjective.

- Hypothetical dilemma responses may not reflect real-life reasoning.

Sex differences in children's friendship

Relationships between boys are **extensive** — boys spend time in a large group and focus on shared activities. Relationships between girls are **intensive** — girls have intimate friendships in pairs and focus on emotional closeness. These differences continue into adolescence. Benenson and Christakos (2003) found that among 10–15-year-olds, girls had more 'best friends', boys' friendships lasted longer and girls worried more about friendship.

Study: Benenson (1990)

Benenson interviewed 10-year-olds and used rating scales to determine important aspects of friendship. The boys' data revealed friendships of large interconnected groups, with the focus on the status of the group. The girls' data revealed more intimate friendships or 'cliques'. Benenson concluded that social networks are different for boys and girls.

Study: Lever (1976)

Lever interviewed 10-year-old US boys and girls about their friendships. Girls preferred a best friend, were happy to show affection and shared intimate secrets. They were also more anxious about threats to friendships and more likely to be jealous. Boys' friendships were more open and more group-focused.

Popularity and rejection

Coie and Dodge (1983) identified five types of child: popular, average, controversial, neglected and rejected. Rejected children can be divided into two types (Berk, 2003):

- **rejected-aggressive** — impulsive, aggressive, hyperactive and lacking in ability to understand others
- **rejected-withdrawn** — passive, socially withdrawn, high in social anxiety and often targeted for bullying

Causes

- **Similarity**. Children choose friends who are similar in terms of sex, age, background etc. Unusual/deviant children tend to be excluded. Kandel (1978) found that friendships lasted longer if the friends were similar.
- **Attractiveness**. Children prefer attractive peers, with the effect more marked in girls than boys (Vaughn and Langlois, 1983). Attractiveness may be physical or linked to status, such as being good at sport.
- **Personality**. Rejected children are aggressive and disruptive. Dodge (1983) found a link between children's personality traits and their popularity.
- **Early relationships**. According to the internal working model, the earliest bond between child and carer acts as a model for future relationships. Perhaps unpopular and rejected children had unsatisfactory early relationships and lack an appropriate internal working model.
- **Poor social skills**.

> ### Study: Dodge et al. (1983)
> Dodge et al. observed playground behaviour, watching a third child trying to join in with a pair already playing together. Popular children were socially adept and able to join in. Neglected children did not attempt to join in and rejected children were too aggressive and forceful.

Evaluation

- A clear cause-and-effect relationship cannot easily be established. Rejection may cause aggression rather than the other way round.
- Learning social skills can help avoid rejection (Oden and Asher, 1977).

Consequences

Rejected children are more likely to have psychiatric problems as adults (Cowen et al., 1973), experience alcoholism (Duck, 1991) and get into trouble with the law (Kuperschmidt and Coie, 1990).

Evaluation

- A cause-and-effect relationship between rejection and negative consequences cannot be determined.
- Schaffer (1996) suggests that aggressiveness may be the key factor rather than rejection.

■ Most studies fail to distinguish between rejection and friendlessness. Bagwell et al. (1998) argued that rejection by some is less damaging than total friendlessness.

Cognitive development

Piaget's theory of cognitive development

Summary specification content
Schemas: adaptation, assimilation and accommodation. Piaget's stages of intellectual development. Characteristics of these stages, including object permanence, conservation, egocentrism, class inclusion. Piaget's research, including the three mountains experiment and conservation experiments.

Piaget used a clinical interview technique to study children's responses to problems. He found that children think in different ways at different ages.

Schemas, adaptation, assimilation and accommodation
A **schema** is a unit of knowledge. Piaget proposed that babies are born with simple schemas, for example sucking and grasping schemas. Infants soon develop new schemas, such as throwing schemas.

The process of developing schemas in response to experience of the world is called **adaptation**. Adaptation occurs through two processes:
- **(1) assimilation** — adding to an existing schema or applying an existing schema to a new situation
- **(2) accommodation** — altering a schema or developing a new schema to cope with a new situation

Piaget referred to **disequilibrium**, which is a state of cognitive imbalance that is experienced when what we know about the world is inconsistent with incoming information. Cognitive balance or **equilibrium** is restored through accommodation. Piaget was a **constructivist**: he believed that understanding of the world is constructed through experience and discovery. He thought that children learned through active discovery and his theory of **discovery learning** was influential in primary education.

Piaget's stages of intellectual development and his research
Piaget proposed four **invariant** and **universal** stages of cognitive development. The child's understanding is different at each stage:
- **(1)** 0–2 years — the sensori-motor stage
- **(2)** 2–7 years — the pre-operational stage
- **(3)** 7–12 years — the concrete operational stage
- **(4)** over 12 years — the formal operational stage

The sensori-motor stage

Knowledge is limited to simple motor reflexes and sensations. There is no **object concept** — the child has no awareness of objects outside the immediate present. Early in the sensori-motor stage there is no distinction between self and others. Intentional behaviour begins at about 8 months and by the end of this stage **general symbolic function** is acquired, so the child understands that one thing can stand for another. **Object permanence (object concept)** arises at around 8 months. This is the understanding that objects continue to exist even when they are out of sight.

Study: Piaget (1963)

Piaget tested object permanence by taking a toy from the child and hiding it under a blanket. Before 8 months of age, infants would not reach for the hidden toy. Infants over 8 months would search for the toy, showing that they had object permanence. Piaget concluded that object permanence develops at around 8 months.

Evaluation

- Failure to reach for the toy may not mean that the infants did not understand that it still existed: they might have thought that it was not allowed or have lacked motor skills.

- Other studies showed that even 3-month-old babies have object permanence. Bower and Wishart (1972) turned out the lights and found that infants continued to reach for an object in the dark.

The pre-operational stage

Pre-operational children cannot perform many cognitive tasks. They cannot perform logical operations (mental tasks). This stage is sometimes divided into two sub-stages: the pre-conceptual (2–4 years) and the intuitive (4–7 years). Typical thinking errors include animism (attributing feelings to inanimate objects), centration (the ability to think about only one feature at a time) and **egocentrism** (the inability to think about something from another person's point of view). Piaget's **three mountains experiment** illustrates egocentrism.

Study: Piaget and Inhelder (1956)

Piaget and Inhelder showed 4–12-year-olds a model of three mountains. A doll was placed somewhere on the model. From the other side of the model the child had to choose the view that the doll would be able to see. Children aged 4–5 years chose their own view but by 7–8 years they could choose the correct view. Piaget concluded that pre-operational children cannot **decentre**: they are **egocentric**.

Study: Hughes (1978)

Hughes showed 3½–5-year-olds a model with intersecting walls. A boy doll and a policeman doll were positioned in the model and the child had to say if the policeman could see the boy. They then had to hide the boy doll from the policeman doll. Hughes found that 90% of children were successful.

Evaluation

- The task was unrealistic. Borke's (1975) child-friendly version used television characters and even 3- or 4-year-olds could give the correct answer.

- Piaget underestimated children's ability. Hughes showed that decentring occurs sooner than Piaget had thought.

Conservation is the ability to understand that the properties of objects or materials stay the same, even though outward appearance may change. This occurs because thinking is ruled by appearance. Piaget's **conservation experiments** involved volume, mass and number.

Study: Piaget and Szeminska (1941)

Piaget and Szeminska showed children two identical containers, each holding the same amount of liquid. They asked each child individually whether there was the same amount in each container or whether one had more. They then poured the liquid from one container into a different tall, thin container. The same question was asked again (post-transformation question). Most children under 7 years replied that the tall, thin container had more liquid. The over-7-year-olds gave the correct answer. It seems that the ability to conserve arises at around 7 years.

Evaluation

- The use of the word 'more' may have confused the children. Perhaps they think of 'more' as 'higher' or 'fuller'.

- Asking the same question twice was confusing. Children might have given a different answer the second time because they thought that the first answer was wrong. Rose and Blank (1974) omitted the first question and found 6-year-olds performed better. McGarrigle and Donaldson's (1974) version with Naughty Teddy showed 60% of 6-year-olds could conserve if the rearrangement of the materials (beads) appeared to be accidental.

- The original studies have been described as lacking 'human sense'.

The concrete operational stage

At 7 years old the child starts to perform mental operations (logical thinking) and is able to conserve. One operation is **reversibility** — the ability to mentally reverse actions, for example the transformation of material in a conservation study. At this stage, logical thinking is limited to concrete problems. The child can perform **conservation** tasks and **class inclusion** tasks. Class inclusion involves understanding the relationship between an overall category and sub-categories.

Study: Piaget and Szeminska (1941)

Piaget and Szeminska tested understanding of overall classes and sub-classes using 20 wooden beads (18 brown and 2 white). Children were asked three questions: Are the beads all wooden? Are there more brown beads or more white beads? Are there more brown beads or more wooden beads? Children under 7 years answered the third question incorrectly, whereas over 7 years they answered it correctly because they could distinguish between the overall class (beads) and the sub-class (brown beads).

Evaluation

- The class inclusion questions are unusual and confusing.

- Making the question more accessible produced different results. In McGarrigle's cow version, 48% of 6-year-olds could complete the task.

The formal operational stage

Children can now think **abstractly** and **hypothetically**. Formal operational thought is more **flexible** than concrete operational thought. Formal operational thinkers can use **hypothetico-deductive reasoning** and **systematic hypothesis testing**.

Study: Inhelder and Piaget (1958)

Inhelder and Piaget used the pendulum problem to test formal operational reasoning. They found that formal operational thinkers varied each factor systematically, changing one variable at a time and enabling them to correctly conclude which factors affected the rate of the pendulum swing. They concluded that systematic problem-solving is a feature of formal operational thinking.

Evaluation of Piaget's theory and methods

- Piaget's stages were criticised as too rigid. He later proposed 'horizontal décalage' where a child may straddle more than one stage.

- His sequence of development has been confirmed in several cultures, although children from non-industrialised societies reach the stages later.

- Not all adults demonstrate formal operational thinking.

- Discovery learning may not be sufficient: Vygotsky argued that adult guidance is also essential.

- The sample was small and unrepresentative, his records lacked detail and the research was not strictly controlled.

- The tasks were confusing and Piaget assumed that a lack of success meant a lack of ability.

- Gelman (1969) found that conservation was almost impossible to teach, supporting Piaget's ideas about readiness.

- Piaget's child-centred approach had a huge effect on education.

- The clinical interview method yielded rich qualitative information, which stimulated much research.

Alternative approaches to children's cognition

Summary specification content

Vygotsky and cognitive development within a social and cultural context. Vygotsky's zone of proximal development. Scaffolding. Guided participation in sociocultural activity.

Nativist explanations and early infant abilities, including knowledge of the physical world (Baillargeon).

The information processing approach: Seigler's research into problem-solving strategies.

Vygotsky and cognitive development

Vygotsky's theory was **sociocultural.** He said that cognitive development was influenced by the social world and culture. Vygotsky thought that children needed to develop the cognitive tools (e.g. language, number systems) of their culture. He proposed that children **internalise** the knowledge of others and learn through social experiences. He saw the child as an **apprentice**.

Zone of proximal development

The zone of proximal development (ZPD) is the difference or distance between what a child can do alone and what he or she can achieve with help. The ZPD considers **potential**, not just current ability.

> ### Study: Hedegaard (1996)
> Hedegaard used a special teaching method to extend children's abilities through their ZPD. Learning activities were designed on three interrelated topics. The children had to integrate the different sets of information to answer questions. Careful structuring of activities enabled whole-class groups of children to work towards their individual potential and through their ZPD.

Scaffolding

Scaffolding involves help and support from an adult or more able peer. Help is gradually withdrawn until the child is independently competent. Scaffolding can occur in many contexts with parents, siblings, older peers and teachers. It has been found to occur in many cultures.

> ### Study: Wood and Middleton (1975)
> Wood and Middleton observed parents helping young children build bricks. The task was too hard for the children to do alone. Parents initially showed their child, then stopped giving direct help but made comments and suggestions. The amount of help was reduced over time.

Evaluation

- This study shows scaffolding of a specific task but this does not show that scaffolding occurs with more general understanding, for example of concepts.

Guided participation in sociocultural activity

Scaffolding of cultural traditions and practices is known as guided participation (Rogoff et al., 1995). Adults model an activity and guide the child in his or her efforts. The child finally reconstructs the knowledge and adopts his or her own version. Rogoff believed that cognitive development is dependent on environment and culture.

> **Study: Rogoff (1995)**
> Rogoff studied the transmission of knowledge in the annual Girl Scout Cookie Sale in the USA. More experienced members of the community passed on knowledge of the event and gave advice and practical help. This knowledge was then reformulated as the girls found new ways of working.

Language

Vygotsky believed that language was a key factor in cognitive development. He stated that monologues enabled a child to plan behaviour. At first these are out loud, then, at around the age of 7, they become internalised (i.e. thought).

Evaluation

- Vygotsky's theory suggests acceleration of cognitive development is possible. Some studies show acceleration is difficult (Gelman, 1969).

- Adult instruction can sometimes be confusing and too much instruction may result in a lack of initiative.

- Vygotsky's ideas have educational applications (e.g. peer tutoring, collective argumentation, community of enquiry).

> **Study: Elbers and Streefland (2000)**
> Elbers and Streefland tested the effectiveness of a community of enquiry in a Dutch school. Teachers and pupils played the role of researcher during maths activities. Teachers gave no explicit instruction but simply rephrased children's comments, correcting errors. The children cooperated well, used evidence constructively and were highly productive.

Nativist explanations and early infant abilities

Nativists believe we are born with **innate** structures determining cognitive ability and that developmental change is due to genetic predisposition. This contrasts with Piaget's constructivist view of cognitive development as a result of active experience.

Knowledge of the physical world

Certain abilities such as **depth perception** may be innate. Bower et al. (1970) found that young infants could perceive an object looming towards them. Gibson and Walk (1960) found that babies aged 6–14 months could perceive depth in a 'visual cliff' experiment.

Baillargeon challenged Piaget's views on object permanence. She devised experiments where infants were presented with **impossible events**. If children showed surprise, this suggested that they had a mental representation of what ought to occur and had object permanence. One study involved a truck rolling down a slope; the other involved a carrot passing behind a screen. In the truck study, Baillargeon found that 6–8-month-olds showed object permanence. In the carrot study, this ability was demonstrated even earlier.

Study: Baillargeon (1991)

Three-month-old babies watched tall and short carrots move from left to right behind a screen. They then saw the same procedure with a screen that had a window in the top half. The tall carrot should have been visible in the window but the researchers made the event 'impossible', with the tall carrot not visible in the window. Babies looked longer in the tall-carrot condition than the short-carrot condition, showing they had object permanence.

Evaluation

- Baillargeon's studies contradict Piaget's views about object permanence and possibly support a nativist view.

The information processing approach

According to this approach, human processing is like the processing of a computer. Research is concentrated on individual cognitive processes. Information processing theorists believe that age-related changes are due to increased **cognitive efficiency**. Bee (1997) suggests that with age there is greater processing efficiency and capacity, the development of rules and the development of **metacognition** (an awareness of one's own cognitive abilities).

Study: Flavell et al. (1996)

Flavell et al. investigated memory strategies used by children aged 5–10 years. Few of the younger children used the strategy of verbal repetition when told to remember pictures. In contrast, most of the older children used this strategy. Flavell concluded that information processing strategies change with age.

Siegler's research into problem-solving strategies

Siegler (1976) proposed that cognitive development involves the acquisition of rules or strategies for solving problems. With age these rules become more complex and can be applied to different problems.

Study: Siegler (1976)

Siegler used a balance scale task with 5–17-year-olds to find out if information processing strategies changed as children got older. On each trial different weights were positioned at different places on a fulcrum. The child had to predict whether the scale would tip and, if so, which way. Before the trials Siegler identified four increasingly complex strategies. Children used the more complex (and successful) strategies as they got older.

- Siegler found that children given feedback began to use more complex strategies, so experience may be more relevant than age.

Siegler (1996) proposed that problem-solving strategies overlap and children choose which strategy to use at any one time. The **overlapping waves** theory has been used in computer simulations of developing cognitive processes.

Evaluation of the information processing approach

- Studies of processes like memory help us to understand developmental changes in processing.

- Information processing findings can inform new teaching techniques.

- Information processing findings can be linked to biological research into brain function.

- The view is not as comprehensive as Piaget's theory of cognitive development.

Comparing Piaget with alternative approaches

Be ready to compare Piaget's theory with the alternative approaches (Table 2).

Table 2 Comparing Piaget's theory

Piaget	Vygotsky
Cognitive development depends on self-discovery	Cognitive development depends on guidance and support from others
Knowledge develops through an inbuilt tendency to adaptation — child is a 'lone scientist'	Knowledge develops through sociocultural interaction — child is an 'apprentice' to more experienced peers
Sees language as incidental or a by-product of cognitive development	Sees language as critical for cognitive development
Increased understanding occurs when child is ready (the readiness approach) and cannot be accelerated	Cognitive understanding can be increased and accelerated through instruction and guidance

Moral development

Piaget and Kohlberg

Summary specification content

Piaget's stages of moral development: pre-moral judgement, moral realism and moral relativism. Kohlberg's pre-conventional, conventional and post-conventional levels. The stages within these levels.

Ways of investigating moral development including the use of moral comparisons and moral dilemmas.

Piaget's stages of moral development

The pre-moral stage

Under 5 years of age the child cannot make sensible moral judgements.

The moral realism stage

Between 5 and 9 years of age, moral judgements are based on other's views of right and wrong (**heteronomous**) and on **consequences** rather than **intention**. Rules are seen as inflexible moral absolutes. Right and wrong are seen as objective reality rather than opinion and there is a belief that wrongdoing should be heavily punished (**expiatory punishment**). Unpleasant events that occur after wrongdoing are seen as punishments (**immanent justice**).

The moral relativism stage

Over 10 years of age, judgement is based on an internalised moral code (**autonomous**). Both intention and consequence are relevant. Rules are no longer seen as fixed, but can be changed. Moral judgement is seen to be a matter of subjective opinion and punishment should be **reciprocal** (reflect the nature of the crime).

Piaget thought that progress through these three stages depended on (a) declining **egocentrism** (allowing for the taking of other people's perspectives) and (b) the ability to **decentre** (allowing for the consideration of several issues at a time).

Evaluation

- Evidence suggests that older children focus more on intention than younger children (Berk, 2003).

- Piaget's theory assumes that moral understanding is fixed at 10 years, but others suggest it continues to develop into adulthood.

- Even adults judge by consequence rather than by intention on occasions.

- The findings were based on research with a limited sample.

- Piaget underestimated children's ability. Nelson (1980) and Helwig et al. (2001) found that 3-year-olds could consider intention.

Piaget's moral comparisons

Children heard two separate stories. In one story, a child causes a lot of damage by accident (breaks 15 cups). In another story, a child causes a small amount of intentional damage (breaks one cup). Piaget asked which boy was naughtier and why. He found that children aged under 10 years thought that the child in the story with most damage was naughtier, whereas children aged 10 years and over considered the intention.

Evaluation

- The moral comparison task places great demand on memory.

- The stories manipulate two variables at once. Nelson (1980) systematically varied the extent of damage and the intention. Where intention was clear, even 3-year-olds considered both intention and consequence.

Piaget's work on telling lies

Piaget found that younger children thought that 'big', absurd lies were naughtier than 'small' lies involving less distortion from the truth. He found older children considered not just whether the statement is false, but also intent to deceive.

Piaget's work on understanding of rules

Piaget (1932) watched children playing marbles and asked them about the rules. Children aged 4–5 did not seem to understand the rules; at 6–9 years they could follow rules but sometimes cheated — they believed that rules were fixed by a higher authority. By 10 years they understood that the rules could be changed by common consent.

Kohlberg's theory of moral development and the moral dilemma technique

Kohlberg (1969) extended Piaget's work. He used the **moral dilemma technique** in which the participant hears a story about a person faced with a choice between two courses of action, each in some way immoral. The most famous was the 'Heinz' dilemma. Heinz has to choose between stealing a drug to save his dying wife and not stealing the drug, thereby allowing her to die. After listening to the story, participants were asked a series of questions in a structured interview, for example 'Should Heinz steal the drug?' and 'Why/why not?' Verbal responses were categorised according to level or stage of moral reasoning. The dilemma technique was used by Kohlberg and later by others such as Eisenberg.

Study: Kohlberg (1963)

Kohlberg used the dilemma technique with 72 boys. They were interviewed every 3 years for 20 years (Colby et al., 1983). Younger boys reasoned on the basis of possible punishment, whereas older boys reasoned on the basis of care, the law and opinions of society. Kohlberg concluded that moral reasoning becomes more complex with age and that it develops in six stages.

Study: Walker et al. (1987)

Walker et al. compared hypothetical and real-life moral reasoning. Adults and children were interviewed about three of Kohlberg's dilemmas and one real-life personal dilemma. Most participants were at the same stage of moral reasoning for the hypothetical and real-life dilemmas. Walker concluded that hypothetical dilemma responses reflect real-life moral reasoning.

Evaluation

- Dilemmas may be too difficult.

- The situations are not real-life, so the technique lacks ecological validity.

- The technique may not have predictive validity, although Kohlberg (1975) found consistency increased between hypothetical and real-life reasoning as people progressed up the stages.

- The technique may be measuring education rather than moral reasoning.

- Analysis may be subjective. However, Kohlberg established high inter-rater reliability using detailed instructions.
- Participants may respond differently on different occasions.

Kohlberg's levels and stages of moral reasoning

According to Kohlberg, the six-stage sequence is **invariant** and **irreversible**.

The pre-conventional level

(1) **Punishment stage** — reasoning is based on whether or not an action would be punished.
(2) **Reward stage** — reasoning is based on whatever benefits the individual (**instrumental gain**).

The conventional level

(3) **Good-boy, good-girl stage** — judgements are based on what other people would approve or disapprove of.
(4) **Law and order stage** — moral choices reflect obedience to authority and adherence to the law.

The post-conventional level

(5) **Social contract stage** — decisions involve the consideration of unique circumstances and basic human rights. There is recognition that laws are not always fair.
(6) **Ethical principle stage** — decisions are governed by self-chosen ethical principles that are seen to be more important than the law.

Study: Walker (1989)

Walker investigated Kohlberg's theory of an invariant and irreversible sequence of development. Participants were tested using dilemmas over 2 years. The responses were scored and categorised according to Kohlberg's stages. Over the 2 years, 37% of participants moved to the next stage, 6% regressed and none skipped a stage.

Evaluation

- Turiel (1978) criticised the distinct stages, proposing different moral domains with moral reasoning differing according to the domain.
- Stage 6 was abandoned in 1975.
- Moral reasoning may not tally with behaviour (Hartshorne and May, 1928).
- Cross-cultural work generally supports Kohlberg's stage sequence (Berk, 2003), although the scoring system may reflect Western values.
- Gilligan (1982) thought that Kohlberg neglected female moral development. She suggested women's answers were more empathic (stage 3), whereas men's answers focused on rights and law (stage 4). Walker et al. (1987) found no sex differences using Kohlberg's scoring system.

Alternatives to Piaget and Kohlberg

Summary specification content

Eisenberg's model of pro-social reasoning, including hedonistic, needs, approval, self-reflective and internalised orientations.

Gilligan's ethic of care: differences between boys and girls. Gilligan's three levels of moral development.

Damon's research into distributive justice.

Psychodynamic explanations of moral development. The role of the superego.

Eisenberg's model of pro-social reasoning

Eisenberg (1983) used **pro-social dilemmas**, for example the 'birthday party' dilemma.

> ### Study: Eisenberg et al. (1987)
> In a longitudinal study, Eisenberg et al. interviewed children aged between 4 and 12 years about pro-social dilemmas. Pre-school and nursery children were **hedonistic** (put their own interests and pleasures before the needs of others). Older children were **empathic** (focused on the feelings of others).

Eisenberg proposed five levels, similar to Kohlberg's stages:

(1) **hedonistic** — correct action is that which benefits self
(2) **needs-oriented** — correct action is that which considers others' needs
(3) **approval-oriented** — correct action is that which would be approved of
(4) **self-reflective (empathic)** — correct action involves sympathy and role-taking
(5) **strongly internalised** — correct action is based on clear values of dignity and respect

Evaluation

- The pattern of change parallels Kohlberg.

- Pro-social reasoning is often more advanced than reasoning about wrongdoing.

- Eisenberg was the first to consider pro-social reasoning.

- Some cross-cultural evidence confirms the levels (Boehnke et al., 1989).

Gilligan's ethic of care: differences between boys and girls

Gilligan (1982) argued that Kohlberg placed more importance on justice-based reasoning than on care-based reasoning and was biased in favour of males. She also criticised Kohlberg's use of male participants. Gilligan said that women's reasoning is as complex as men's, but different; women focus on relationships and care (morality of care) and men focus on rights and law (morality of justice):

- **morality of care** — concern about the effect of actions on the feelings and needs of others
- **morality of justice** — concern about whether or not rules have been broken and appropriate punishment

Study: Gilligan (1977)

Gilligan used unstructured interviews with 29 women considering abortion. She found they focused on responsibility and feelings (Kohlberg's stage 3) rather than justice. She therefore proposed three levels of female morality.

Gilligan's three levels of moral development

(1) **self-interest** — focus on what is best for self
(2) **self-sacrifice** — focus on the welfare of others rather than one's own needs
(3) **non-violence or universal care** — focus on the importance of not hurting others

Study: Walker (1989)

Walker tested people on hypothetical and real-life dilemmas, scoring responses using both Kohlberg's stages and Gilligan's levels. Both male and female participants were found to use care-based and justice-based orientations. This study confirmed that there were no substantial sex differences in moral reasoning.

Evaluation

- Some studies show no sex differences in moral judgement. The kind of reasoning may depend more on the type of dilemma than on the sex of the participant (Walker, 1989).

- Gilligan only interviewed women. Men may have used similar arguments in their reasoning about abortion.

Damon's research into distributive justice

Damon (1977) studied reasoning about how things should be fairly divided (**distributive justice**) and found it became more sophisticated with age. Young children reason on the basis of **personal gain**. At around 5 years, there is a fixed idea of **equality** and equal shares, ignoring differences in effort. By 7 years, reasoning is based on **merit**. By 8–9 years, reasoning is based on **benevolence**, with special consideration for the disadvantaged.

Study: Damon (1977)

Damon asked children aged 4–10 years how they would share money from a picture sale. The youngest children thought that they should have the most. The 5–7-year-olds wanted to share the profit equally. Over 7 years they considered individual effort and need. Damon concluded that distributive justice shifts from focus on self to focus on fairness and others.

- Damon offered a different view on moral development.

- Findings generally reflect changes observed by Kohlberg and Eisenberg.

- Cross-cultural findings support Damon's results.

- The distributive justice dilemmas are realistic for children.

Psychodynamic explanations of moral development

Psychodynamic theory focuses on the emotional aspect of morality. Freud (1923) thought that morality is acquired in the phallic stage of psychosexual development at around 4–6 years.

The role of the superego

Freud proposed three parts to the personality: id, ego and superego. The superego is responsible for morality. It develops through the resolution of the Oedipus/Electra complex in the phallic stage. It acts as an internal parent or **conscience**, punishing us with guilt if we behave badly. It also includes the **ego-ideal**, which indicates high moral standards. The superego represents the parent's values and standards.

The Oedipus complex

At 5 years of age the boy desires his mother and fears castration by his father. To resolve the conflict the boy gives up the desire for the mother and identifies with the father (the aggressor), internalising the father's moral values (the superego).

The Electra complex

Believing she has already been castrated, the girl identifies with the mother, internalising her moral values (the superego). According to Freud, females do not identify as strongly as males because girls are less afraid than boys. Freud therefore believed that women are morally inferior.

- There is no evidence that the superego exists.

- Children understand right and wrong before 5 years of age (Nelson, 1980) and moral reasoning continues to develop after 5 years.

- The view of women as morally inferior is not supported (Hoffman, 1975).

- Children without a same-sex parent do not appear to be any less moral.

- According to social learning theory, moral behaviour is influenced by peers, role models etc. and not just the same-sex parent.

Applied options
Cognition and law

Recognising and remembering faces

Summary specification content
Processes involved in recognition of faces. Explanations for face recognition, including feature analysis and holistic forms.

The construction of likenesses using composite systems.

Identification procedures: simultaneous and sequential line-ups.

Processes involved in recognition of faces
Identification is looking at a face and knowing who it is; recognition is knowing we have seen a face before; recall is describing (or drawing) a face from memory. Recognition is easier than identification, and memory for faces seems to deteriorate over time.

Explanations for face recognition
You need to know two theories — **feature analysis theory** and **holistic forms theory** — and should be able to evaluate and compare them.

Feature analysis theory
This is a **bottom-up** or **data-driven** theory of information processing, which states that incoming visual cues (facial features) drive recognition. Some studies show features are important. Ellis et al. (1979) found that we rely more on external facial features such as hair and face shape to recognise less familiar people and internal features to recognise faces of more familiar people.

> **Study: Woodhead et al. (1979)**
> Woodhead et al. studied the use of a training course in feature-based face recognition. Participants trained to recognise individual facial features were less able to identify a target face than controls, suggesting simple feature analysis is not so important for face recognition.

Evaluation

- Basic bottom-up information (a face with features) is essential for recognition.

- Bottom-up processing is unlikely to explain face recognition completely: other factors such as expression are probably important.

- Individual features cannot be recognised out of context (Tanaka and Farah, 1993).

- Feature theory cannot explain why faces are harder to recognise if configuration is altered.

Holistic form theory

This is a **top-down** theory which states that previously stored semantic information is important for face recognition (Bruce and Young, 1986). We recognise a face as a **whole**, analysing not just features but also **configuration**, feelings and **semantic information**. For each face we have seen before, we have a stored **template**:
- stage 1: structural encoding — the visual structure of the face is analysed
- stage 2: face recognition unit (FRU) triggered, like a pattern or template
- stage 3: personal identity node (PIN) triggered, which includes semantic information about the person
- stage 4: name generation

Study: Young and Hay (1986)

Young and Hay showed participants faces cut across horizontally, recording recognition times for each separate half. Two non-matching halves were put together to make a composite face and participants had to name the people in the two halves. Recognition time was greater when the two were in a composite that seemed to produce a completely new holistic face. This shows features are less important for recognition than wholes.

Other studies show how changing the layout leads to longer recognition time: Haig (1984) altered the spacing between features; Yin (1969) inverted faces.

Study: Tanaka and Farah (1993)

Tanaka and Farah showed how it was difficult to identify single features in isolation. Participants learned to recognise a face and could then tell if the face was presented with a different nose from the original. However, they could not distinguish between the original nose and the new nose when the noses were presented out of context (without the face), supporting the holistic theory.

Prosopagnosia and **Capgras syndrome** are disorders of face recognition. Both show that face recognition involves cognition and emotion, suggesting it may be holistic.

Study: Young et al. (1985)

Young et al. asked participants to keep a diary of face recognition events. Content analysis showed that people's recognition experiences confirmed Bruce and Young's four-stage sequence — no one reported being able to name someone without first knowing other things about them.

Evaluation

- Evidence supports the Bruce and Young sequence and the importance of configuration.
- The theory acknowledges the role of emotion and semantic information.
- The theory has been elaborated using computer modelling (Burton et al., 1990).

Construction of likenesses using composite systems

A composite system involves constructing a face from separate features (e.g. identikit, photo-fit, e-fit). First-generation systems were paper-based. Nowadays they are computerised, eliminating the obvious lines between features and allowing for feature blending and changes in spacing. Early systems were not always effective. Second-generation systems use computers to draw a composite based on verbal description, adding 'standard' features where there are gaps.

Study: Ellis et al. (1978)

Ellis et al. compared the accuracy of an early photo-fit system with hand-drawn sketches. Working from memory, the photo-fit system was more accurate than the sketch. However, with the target face present, the sketches were judged to be more accurate than photo-fits.

Evaluation

- Early systems were limited.

- New-generation systems are more effective (Davies et al., 2000).

- Kapardis (1997) found that the FACE system enabled confirmation of a suspect in 23% of cases.

- Studies lack ecological validity. In real life witnesses do not have time to study the face, and the person using the likeness to identify a suspect will probably know the suspect (e.g. work colleague, neighbour).

Identification procedures: simultaneous and sequential line-ups

UK identity parades usually involve a real suspect and eight 'foils'. In a **simultaneous** line-up, the witness sees all members of the line-up together. This may lead to a **relative judgement** about which person is most like the suspect. According to Wells et al. (1998), witnesses assume the suspect must be in the line-up and will choose someone even if they are unsure, increasing the chance of false identification. Malpass and Devine (1981) found that telling witnesses that a culprit may or may not be present significantly reduces false identifications.

Lindsay and Wells (1985) introduced the **sequential** line-up, where possible suspects are seen one at a time and the witness has to make an **absolute judgement** about each.

Study: Steblay et al. (2001)

Steblay et al. analysed 30 studies comparing simultaneous and sequential line-ups. They found that a suspect was more likely to be identified in simultaneous line-ups, even when the culprit was not actually present. In the most realistic studies, sequential line-ups resulted in a similar number of correct identifications and fewer false identifications.

Many line-ups now use a video system (e.g. the **VIPER** system — Kemp et al., 2001) where witnesses see a video sequence of the suspect among eight videos of foils. The

VIPER system is sequential and highly controlled, and has legal equivalence with traditional line-ups.

Evaluation

- Sequential line-ups reduce the chance of false identifications.

- Video line-ups are increasingly used to avoid problems of control.

- Other factors that affect identification procedures include similarity of foils, unintentional cues from the police officer, feedback (witnesses who are told that their identification was correct become more confident about their choice).

Recalling events

Summary specification content

Factors affecting the reliability of eyewitness accounts and eyewitness identification, including post-event contamination. Improving eyewitness recall, including features of the cognitive interview. Children as eyewitnesses. Flashbulb memory: memory for shocking events.

The false memory debate. Controversy surrounding the recovery of repressed memories. The existence of false memories. Evidence relating to repression and false memory. Ethical and theoretical implications of the false memory debate.

Bartlett used the 'War of the Ghosts' study to show how recall involves '**effort after meaning**', suggesting that memories are actively altered to fit with our existing **schema**; memory is active, **reconstructive** and can involve **confabulation**. This means that eyewitness identification is likely to be unreliable and for this reason courts are careful not to assume single eyewitness accounts are reliable (Devlin Report, 1976).

Factors affecting the reliability of eyewitness accounts

These include post-event contamination, emotion/stress, weapon focus, context and expectations/stereotypes.

Post-event contamination

This happens when a witness's memory of an event is altered after the event either by questioning or through discussion. Loftus et al. (1970s) found that **leading questions** influence recall. For example, Loftus and Palmer (1974) showed how changing the word 'smashed' and 'hit' in a question about a car crash led to differing estimates of speed (40.8 and 34 miles per hour).

> **Study: Loftus (1975)**
> Loftus showed participants a car accident on film and asked either 'How fast was the white sports car going when it passed the stop sign?' or 'How fast was the white sports car going when it passed the barn?' In the film there was a stop sign, but no barn. Significantly more participants reported seeing a barn in the second condition.

Another source of post-event contamination is **witness discussion**.

> ### Study: Wright et al. (2000)
> Wright et al. showed participants a picture story about a woman stealing a wallet. In one condition the woman was alone; in the other, she had an accomplice. Pairs of participants, one from each condition, then discussed the story. After the discussion each participant recalled individually. In 79% of cases, one member of each pair changed their recall (about the accomplice) following discussion.

Emotion/stress
Loftus and Burns (1982) found that participants who viewed a violent version of a video about a bank robbery were less able to recall the critical event. However, Yuille and Cutshall (1986) showed that recall of a real-life incident involving weapons was extremely accurate even months later.

Weapon focus
Loftus et al. (1987) found that witnesses will sometimes attend to a weapon and therefore recall few other details. Participants saw a video of a robbery in which a gun was pointed at the check-out operator. In the control group video, there was no gun. Participants in the 'gun' condition showed poorer recall of the event.

Context
Godden and Baddeley (1975) showed how divers recalled more information if they learnt and recalled it in the same context (i.e. underwater). Malpass and Devine (1981) found that participants given contextual information showed better recall of an act of vandalism than those not given contextual information.

Expectations/stereotypes
Howitt (1991) found that recollections of a story were distorted by racist assumptions and Gruneberg (1992) found that witnesses to a staged mugging often believed that the (female) mugger was male.

Improving eyewitness recall: the cognitive interview
Fisher and Geiselman (1992) proposed the four-feature cognitive interview:
- **(1)** The interviewer reinstates the context.
- **(2)** Witnesses are asked to report every detail.
- **(3)** Events are recalled in a different order.
- **(4)** Events are recalled from different perspectives.

> ### Study: Geiselman et al. (1985)
> Geiselman et al. interviewed participants about a video of a crime using the cognitive interview and a standard interview. Witnesses recalled more items of information using the cognitive interview (41.2 correct items) than the standard interview (29.4 correct items).

- The cognitive interview improves recall except in young children (Geiselman, 1999).
- It is unclear whether all four features are essential (Milne and Bull, 2002).
- The enhancing effect decreases as time between event and interview increases.
- The cognitive interview enhances recall of events but not of people.

Children as eyewitnesses

Child witnesses can be less reliable than adults (Estgate and Groome, 2005). They are more affected by post-event contamination and their memories deteriorate more over time. They have difficulty distinguishing between memories for events they have experienced and memories from elsewhere (**source monitoring**).

Study: Poole and Lindsay (2001)

Poole and Lindsay tested children's ability to recall science demonstrations. They found that 35% of the children confused memory for actual demonstrations with memory for stories they had been told about other demonstrations. They concluded that young children find it difficult to monitor the source of a memory.

Evaluation

- Demand characteristics may be a factor. Ceci and Bruck (1993) suggested that children may give inaccurate details rather than not answer.
- Experiments involve recall of neutral rather than traumatic real-life events.
- Marin et al. (1979) found no difference in accuracy of identification and the effect of leading questions with age.

Flashbulb memory

Flashbulb memories are vivid memories of **shocking** events which include detail of the **context**, such as what we were doing when we heard of the 9/11 twin towers disaster. They are a special kind of **source memory** related to time and place of learning and may be linked to specific neural mechanisms. Some evidence indicates they are resistant to normal forgetting.

Study: Sharot et al. (2007)

Sharot et al. asked participants to recall the 9/11 attacks on the World Trade Center 3 years later. Those closest to the scene and therefore more personally shocked showed selective activation of the amygdala on MRI scans when recalling. Those who were further away did not show the same effect. Sharot concluded that highly arousing flashbulb memories involve a special neural mechanism.

Evaluation

- Flashbulb memories may appear stronger simply because of repeated retrieval.

- Neisser and Harsch (1992) found recall of the *Challenger* space shuttle disaster deteriorated over time.

- Flashbulb memory research suggests that upsetting memories are very vivid indeed.

The false memory debate

A **recovered memory** is where someone recalls an event of which they had no previous knowledge. A **false memory** is memory for an event that never happened. False memory syndrome (FMS) refers to a condition where someone has a memory of a traumatic experience (often childhood abuse) that never happened, but the person believes it did happen.

Controversy surrounding the recovery of repressed memories

Whether or not recovered memories can occur depends on Freud's theory of **repression**. Repression is a defence mechanism by which memories for unpleasant or upsetting events are 'pushed' into the unconscious. Some experimental evidence suggests repression is possible, for example Levinger and Clark (1961) found that participants were less likely to recall emotionally negative word associations that neutral ones.

Study: Williams (1994)

Williams interviewed women about their sexual histories. Although hospital records showed they had been abused as children, 38% of the women did not report the abusive event, suggesting they may have repressed the memories.

Study: Wright et al. (2006)

Wright et al. discussed recovered memory cases and argued that it is often uncertain (a) that the original event really happened, (b) that there was a time when the person could not consciously recall the event, and (c) whether eventual recall was actually spontaneous or a product of suggestion.

Evaluation

- Recovered memories may be a product of suggestion.

- Repression is unconscious so cannot be properly investigated.

- Memory in experiments is not like real-life memory for traumatic events.

- Williams's participants may have chosen not to discuss events they could remember.

The existence of false memories

False memories may be due to **reconstruction**. Loftus (2001) argued that people may begin to believe an event happened simply because a therapist uses guided imagination. Loftus and Ketcham (1994) showed memories can be **implanted** by suggestion.

Study: Loftus and Ketcham (1994)

Loftus and Ketcham introduced the idea of being 'lost in a shopping mall' in conversation. The topic was mentioned several times further and participants were asked about the event. Participants gradually became confident that they recalled the event, even giving detail they had not been told.

Study: Lindsay et al. (2004)

Lindsay et al. told students stories about events that had occurred while they were at school. Two events were real; one was fictitious. Around 25% recalled some detail of the fictitious event. With a photograph as a cue, around 33% recalled the fictitious event. This shows that people recall events that never happened, especially when given a cue.

Evaluation

- Events used in laboratory research are not like traumatic real-life memories.

- False memories may be affected by individual differences in suggestibility and meta-memory (awareness of own memory) (Wright et al., 2006).

Ethical and theoretical implications of the false memory debate

As most cases of false or recovered memory involve cases of childhood abuse, there are many **ethical concerns**: someone may be innocent and wrongly accused; family break-up and stigma; trauma for the patient, family and friends.

The **theoretical implications** relate to (a) Freud's psychoanalytic theory in general and the concept of repression, and (b) the theory of memory as active and reconstructive (Bartlett's schema theory and Loftus's work). If unconscious memories can be recovered, this is consistent with Freud's theory. If the memories are false, this fits with Bartlett's and Loftus's reconstructive view.

Schizophrenia and mood disorders

Schizophrenia

Summary specification content

Classification of schizophrenia, including sub-types. Symptoms and diagnosis. Explanations, including biological and cognitive. Sociocultural explanations: labelling and family dysfunction.

Treatments of schizophrenia, including anti-psychotic drugs, behavioural treatments and psychotherapy. The role of community care. Evaluation of these treatments.

Classification of schizophrenia

There are five sub-types:

- **disorganised** (hebephrenic) — disorganised speech, bizarre behaviour
- **catatonic** — excess motor activity or fixed, rigid posture (catatonic stupor)
- **paranoid** — delusions of grandeur/persecution, hallucinations; otherwise apparently normal
- **residual** — social withdrawal and flattened affect (emotion)
- **undifferentiated** — a mixture of symptoms from other sub-types

Evaluation

- The catatonic type is rare and may not be a separate category.

- The undifferentiated category is vague and over-used.

- It is difficult to distinguish between schizophrenia and similar disorders such as schizoaffective disorder.

Symptoms of schizophrenia

Positive symptoms:

- **hallucinations** — perceptions without external stimuli, e.g. hearing voices
- **delusions** — beliefs the sufferer thinks are true, of persecution or grandeur, e.g. 'I am Jesus'.
- **thought and speech disturbances** — unconnected, incoherent, 'word salad', thought insertion/broadcasting
- **disorganised behaviour** — unpredictable, excited or wild behaviour (catatonic excitement)

Negative symptoms:

- avolition (lack of will)
- flattened affect (no emotion)
- social isolation or withdrawal

Secondary symptoms

These are conditions that are a consequence of the disorder, such as depression, anxiety and alcohol abuse.

Study: Kring and Neale (1996)

Kring and Neale observed schizophrenia sufferers and non-sufferers watching emotional films. Schizophrenia sufferers showed less facial expression during the film but reported similar levels of emotional experience afterwards. It seems that people with schizophrenia experience similar emotion but do not show it.

Diagnosis of schizophrenia

Two or more of the following **core symptoms** are required: delusions, hallucinations, disorganised speech, disorganised behaviour, negative symptoms. There should also be poor social/life functioning. Overall, there must be continuous disturbance for at least for 6 months, with core symptoms for at least 1 month. Diagnosis is complicated because schizophrenia has three phases:

(1) prodomal — positive symptoms with normal life functioning

(2) active — strong positive symptoms

(3) residual — negative symptoms only

Diagnosis usually occurs in the active phase.

Evaluation

- Reliability is a problem.

- There may be ethnic bias.

Study: Goater et al. (1999)

Goater et al. monitored people from different ethnic groups for 5 years to see how many were diagnosed with schizophrenia. People from black ethnic minority groups were more likely to be diagnosed with schizophrenia.

Explanations of schizophrenia

The present view is that people may be biologically pre-disposed to the disorder, which can be triggered by stress (**diathesis-stress model).**

Biological explanations

Genetics

Schizophrenia may be **inherited**. Evidence comes from twin, family and adoption studies. Gottesman's (1991) review of more than 40 studies found concordance rates (both individuals in a pair have the disorder) increase as genetic similarity increases: identical (MZ) twins 46%, non-identical (DZ) twins 14% and siblings 10%. A child with one schizophrenic parent has a 1 in 8 chance of developing schizophrenia (Gottesman and Erlenmeyer-Kimling, 2001).

Study: Tienara (1991)

Tienara looked at the rates of schizophrenia in adopted children of mothers diagnosed with schizophrenia and controls whose mothers did not have schizophrenia. Approximately 10% of those with mothers with schizophrenia had schizophrenia, in contrast to 1% of the control group.

Evaluation

- The MZ rate is not 100%, suggesting the environment is also a factor.

- Higher MZ than DZ rates would also be predicted by environmentalists, as MZ pairs have a more shared environment than DZ pairs.

- No single schizophrenia gene has been identified.

- Early twin evidence is unreliable. Diagnosis was less rigorous and supposedly separated pairs were not really separated.

Biochemistry

Schizophrenia may be due to **excess dopamine**, a neurotransmitter. This may cause positive symptoms. Support for the dopamine hypothesis:

- post-mortems of schizophrenia sufferers show high levels of dopamine (Iversen, 1979)
- amphetamines and cocaine affect dopamine function and cause positive symptoms
- antipsychotic drugs (e.g. **chlorpromazine**) reduce dopamine activity and reduce positive symptoms

Evaluation

- Excess dopamine may be a cause or a consequence of the disorder.

- Other neurotransmitters, such as serotonin, are also involved (Breier, 1995).

- Some brain areas (i.e. the hypothalamus and amygdala) show excess dopamine, whereas others show levels below normal (i.e. the prefrontal cortex).

- Excess dopamine does not explain negative symptoms.

Other biological explanations

Schizophrenia sufferers show **brain anomalies**. For example, Weyandt (2006) found enlarged ventricles and Barch (2005) found that the prefrontal cortex is smaller and less active. Exposure of the mother to the **flu virus** in the second trimester has also been linked to schizophrenia in the child (Cannon, 1991).

Cognitive explanations

Schizophrenia may be due to **faulty processing** resulting in disturbed language, thought and perception. Beck and Rector (2005) claim schizophrenia sufferers may perceive their own imaginings as real. Frith (1992) suggested that schizophrenia sufferers attribute their own thoughts to something external, so hearing voices is a misperception of own 'inner speech'. Particular processing problems are linked to **alien control symptoms**, where the sufferer thinks external forces govern their thoughts and actions.

Study: Stirling et al. (1998)

Stirling et al. investigated the ability of patients with schizophrenia to recognise a drawing they had produced with their hand hidden behind a screen. Patients with reality distortion symptoms made more incorrect identifications than controls. This inability to recognise own output indicates faulty information processing.

Evaluation

- Studies show information processing anomalies in people with schizophrenia.

- The cognitive explanation explains the symptoms but not the cause.

- Together with the biological explanation, the cognitive explanation may provide a full account of the disorder.

Sociocultural explanations

Labelling

Szasz (1962) argued that the label 'schizophrenic' becomes a **self-fulfilling prophecy** so the person begins to conform to the label showing more symptoms of the disorder. Rosenhan (1973) showed how, once labelled 'schizophrenic', even normal behaviour tends to be perceived as characteristic of the disorder and the label sticks.

> **Study: Rosenhan (1973)**
>
> Rosenhan asked eight confederates to go to hospital complaining of symptoms of schizophrenia. They were diagnosed and admitted, after which time they behaved completely normally and asked to be released. Hospital staff did not realise they were imposters and interpreted normal behaviours as symptoms. Their average stay was 17 days. They were discharged as 'schizophrenia in remission'.

Family dysfunction

Families of schizophrenia patients show high levels of conflict, communication problems and are highly critical and controlling. Mothers tend to be harsh and critical (**schizophrenogenic**). Bateson et al. (1956) referred to people with schizophrenia as being in a **double bind** or 'no win' situation where the parent's verbal and non-verbal messages conflict, causing the child to withdraw. Relapse is more likely when a recovering patient returns to a family high in **expressed emotion (EE)**. Butzlaff and Hooley (1998) found relapse rates of 70% in high EE families compared to 30% in low EE families.

Evaluation

- Labelling does not explain how the disorder arises in the first place.
- EE may be due to the child's disturbed behaviour rather than a cause.
- Family-based explanations lead to blame.
- The family may be one source of stress in the diathesis-stress model.

Treatments of schizophrenia

Individuals respond differently to different treatments, but the most effective approach is probably a combination of drugs, psychotherapy and community care.

Anti-psychotic drugs

Conventional anti-psychotics are also called **neuroleptics**. **Chlorpromazine** was first used in 1950s. It acts by blocking dopamine receptor sites, reducing dopamine activity and treating positive symptoms.

> **Study: Cole et al. (1964)**
>
> Cole et al. compared drug treatment with a control group. The drug group took chlorpromazine for 6 weeks while the control took a placebo. The drug group showed significant improvement (75%) compared to the placebo group (25%).

Atypical anti-psychotics (e.g. **clozapine**, **risperidone**) are new-generation drugs that reduce both positive and negative symptoms. They affect levels of dopamine and serotonin and are effective with patients who do not improve with conventional anti-psychotics.

Evaluation

- Anti-psychotic drugs reduce the symptoms of schizophrenia.
- The drugs dramatically improve life for sufferers and families.
- One-quarter of patients do not respond to conventional anti-psychotics.
- The drugs must be taken continuously otherwise the symptoms return ('revolving door' syndrome).
- Side effects of conventional anti-psychotics include muscle tremors and tardive dyskinesia (jerky movements of the face and tongue).
- Side effects of new-generation drugs include nausea, weight gain, irregular heartbeat and (occasionally) an autoimmune disorder.

Behavioural treatments

Treatments based on operant conditioning or social learning theory have some effect on reducing bizarre behaviours. **Token economies** have been used in hospitals.

Study: Paul and Lentz (1977)

Paul and Lentz studied a token economy in a hospital. Schizophrenia patients were given tokens for appropriate behaviours. The tokens could be exchanged for meals, cigarettes etc. Over 6 years, positive and negative symptoms reduced. However, when behaviour was no longer reinforced some patients relapsed.

Evaluation

- Token economies modify behaviour but do not treat the underlying disturbances.
- Behavioural treatments can be combined with drug therapy.
- Token systems are ethically questionable as basic rights are withdrawn at the start.

Psychotherapy

Psychoanalytic therapy is of little use for people with schizophrenia as patients have no insight. **Cognitive therapy** (Beck and Rector, 2006) attempts to help change negative attitudes and works on symptoms such as hearing voices. The therapist tries to change the patient's perception from feeling out of control (hearing things) to being in control, regarding the voices as someone trying to talk to them. **Family therapy** aims to increase tolerance, decrease criticism, reduce guilt and improve communication.

Study: Hogarty et al. (1986)

Hogarty et al. compared family therapy with other treatments. Patients received medication only, medication plus social skills training, medication plus family therapy or medication plus social skills training and family therapy. After 1 year, relapse rates were 40% for medication only, 20% for medication plus social skills training or family therapy, 0% for medication plus social skills training and family therapy combined.

- Psychotherapies address different aspects of the disorder.

- Some psychotherapies are not helpful.

- Combined with medication, family therapy seems to work well.

The role of community care

Community care is an alternative to institutional care involving support in the community so sufferers can live as normal a life as possible. It may involve sheltered or supported living arrangements, ongoing therapy and enhancement of social skills.

Study: Stein and Test (1980)

Stein and Test compared the effectiveness of community care for schizophrenia patients over 12 months. One group received hospital treatment with medication and was then discharged without support. The community care group had training in skills and educational support after discharge. Most of the unsupported patients had to be re-admitted to hospital within the year, whereas most of the community care group remained living in the community.

- Adequately supported community care is preferable to the stigma and negative effects of institutionalisation.

- If support is withdrawn, relapse is likely.

- Good community care is expensive.

- Medication needs to be careful monitored.

Mood disorders

Summary specification content

Unipolar and bipolar depression. Seasonal affective disorder (SAD). Symptoms and diagnosis of mood disorders. Explanations, including biological, cognitive, behavioural and psychodynamic.

Treatments of mood disorders, including biological and cognitive.

Evaluation of these treatments.

Unipolar and bipolar depression

With **unipolar depression**, the patient's mood is at the low end of the mood spectrum. Symptoms include:

- **emotional** (e.g. sadness, loss of pleasure and guilt)
- **cognitive** (e.g. poor concentration and memory)
- **physiological** (e.g. sleep disturbances, headaches and tiredness)
- **behavioural** (e.g. social withdrawal and poor hygiene)

Clinical diagnosis of depression requires at least five symptoms for at least 2 weeks. Onset may be gradual or sudden. People who have had one major depressive episode are at risk of further episodes. Depression is twice as likely in women as men (Nolen-Hoeksema, 2002) across all age groups and cultures.

With **bipolar depression**, the patient suffers extreme mood swings between deep depression and **mania**. Mania symptoms include euphoria, highly elevated mood, grand plans, irrational decisions, high energy, rapid speech and little sleep. In the manic phase the person may stop taking medication. After the manic phase there may be deep depression and exhaustion.

Diagnosis of bipolar disorder requires both a major depressive episode and a manic episode. Some 1–2% of adults suffer from bipolar depression, with equal rates for men and women (Shastry, 2005). Onset is usually around 20 years.

Seasonal affective disorder (SAD)

SAD typically occurs in **winter**, most commonly as winter depression without manic episodes. Rarely there is major depression in winter and mania in summer. Symptoms are depression, excess sleep, increased appetite and weight gain. Rates are higher in northerly and southerly countries. Diagnosis requires winter depression for at least 2 years.

> **Study: Terman (1988)**
> Terman studied medical records and found that SAD occurs more often in New Hampshire (10%), where daylight hours are short in winter, than in Florida (2%), where daylight hours are long all year.

Explanations of mood disorders

The biological and cognitive explanations are the strongest for unipolar depression and the biological is the preferred explanation for bipolar depression.

Biological explanations

Genetics

Family/twin studies suggest a genetic basis, with a **family history** increasing the risk of developing the disorder. Twin studies show higher concordance rates for identical (MZ) twins. The genetic contribution in bipolar depression seems to be much higher than in unipolar depression. Research indicates an abnormal serotonin transporter (**SERT**) gene could play a key role (Southwick, 2005)

> **Study: McGuffin (1996)**
> McGuffin studied 177 sets of twins. For **unipolar** depression, the concordance rates were 46% for identical (MZ) twins and 20% for non-identical (DZ) twins, indicating a genetic component.

> **Study: Price (1968)**
> In a study of **bipolar** disorder, Price found concordance of 68% for MZs raised together, 67% for separated MZs and 23% for DZs. These rates indicate a genetic component for bipolar depression.

Study: Madden (2005)

Madden studied concordance rates for **SAD** in over 4500 Australian twin pairs. Concordance rates were 75% for MZs and 50% for DZs, supporting a genetic explanation.

Biochemistry

The neurotransmitters **serotonin** and **norepinephrine** are involved in unipolar and bipolar disorders. Both affect energy levels, sleep, hunger and activity, and are found in the limbic system which controls sleep, appetite and emotions. Low levels cause depression, although it is now thought to be due to an interaction between the two (Thase, 2002). Depression has also been linked to high levels of **cortisol**, which is released by the endocrine system at times of stress. In depressed people the high cortisol level seems to be maintained even after the stressful event has disappeared (Southwick et al., 2005).

In bipolar disorder, serotonin is low in the manic phase and norepinephrine is high (Shastry, 2005). In the depression phase, both are low. Bipolar depression has also been linked to **abnormal ion activity** at the neuronal membrane, resulting in abnormal electrical impulses in the neuron.

SAD is associated with levels of **melatonin**, a brain chemical secreted by the **pineal gland** and produced during the hours of darkness. In winter months melatonin levels increase.

Brain abnormalities

Brain scans suggest abnormality in four areas of the brain may be associated with depression: prefrontal cortex, hippocampus, anterior cingulated cortex and amygdala.

Evaluation

- No single gene for mood disorders has been identified.

- Reserpine (a medication for high blood pressure) reduces levels of serotonin and epinephrine and can cause depression.

- Some research into postnatal depression suggests it is due to social factors rather than hormone changes (Hendrick et al., 1998).

- Brain abnormalities and high or low levels of brain chemicals may be a consequence of depression rather than a cause.

- Twin studies have the same problems as for schizophrenia.

Cognitive explanations

Cognitive psychologists suggest depression is due to negative thinking (Beck, 1987). **Negative schemas** develop in childhood and adolescence. Negative thinking involves:

- **over-generalisation** (one bad thing means everything is bad)
- **magnification/catastrophisation** (blowing up events out of proportion)

- **selective perception** of negative events
- **absolutism** (if things are not perfect, it is a disaster)

Beck proposed the **cognitive triad**, stating that depressed people think negatively about themselves, the world and the future.

Study: Alloy et al. (1999)

Alloy et al. identified students as either 'optimistic' thinkers or 'hopeless' thinkers. The students were interviewed regularly over 2½ years. Only 1% of those with an optimistic thinking style developed depression, compared to 17% of those with a hopeless thinking style.

Study: Beck (1976)

Beck gave the dysfunctional attitude scale (DAS) to depressed and non-depressed people. Those with depression scored higher on the DAS, showing they thought more negatively about events and situations than non-depressed people.

The revised theory of learned helplessness is called the attribution-helplessness model (Peterson and Seligman, 1984; Abramson et al., 2002). The model states that depressed people make internal, stable, global attributions for negative events, i.e. they blame themselves.

Evaluation

- Cognitive explanations are based on research with people.

- Cognitive factors cannot explain the manic phase in bipolar depression.

- Cognitive explanations have led to effective cognitive therapies.

Behavioural explanations

Behaviourists explain depression in terms of **reinforcement**; people with depression are rewarded for negative behaviour. Lewinsohn (1974) explained depression in terms of operant conditioning; loss (e.g. unemployment) leads to a reduction in positive reinforcement, which leads to social withdrawal, which leads to further reduction in positive reinforcement etc. Once someone becomes depressed, this is reinforced via attention from others. The theory of **learned helplessness** (Seligman, 1974) suggests that uncontrollable negative events can lead to depression. Seligman's theory was based on classical conditioning experiments with dogs. Wu et al. (1999) found serotonin and norepinephrine were lower than normal in rats used in learned helplessness experiments.

Study: Seligman (1974)

Seligman subjected dogs to inescapable electric shocks. At first they tried to escape, but then they gave up. Later, when they could escape, they did not try to. They had become helpless. Seligman said this is how people develop depression when they cannot control negative events.

Evaluation

- Animal findings cannot really be generalised to humans.

- Strict behavioural explanations take no account of cognition.

- The theory of learned helplessness was later updated to recognise the role of cognition.

Psychodynamic explanations

Freud (1917) explained depression in terms of grief (**loss**) and **dependency**. Grief as a result of early loss turns to anger, which is turned inward and results in self-blame (**introjection of hostility**). Loss in adulthood brings back feelings of loss experienced as a child, causing depression.

Another psychodynamic explanation is that depression results from failure to meet the excessively high demands of over-harsh parents. In adulthood this leads to depression due to unattainable standards and ideals. Klein et al. (2002) found depression is associated with dependency, perfectionism and low self-esteem.

According to Freud, bipolar depression is due to interaction between the id, ego and superego. When the superego dominates, this causes guilt, leading to depression. The ego tries to control the superego and over-reaction leads to the manic phase.

Evaluation

- There is little scientific evidence, although Bowlby's work on attachment and loss was based on research.

- Psychodynamic explanations have given way to interpersonal theories, such as contingency self-worth theory (Kuiper and Olinger, 1986).

Treatments of mood disorders

For unipolar depression and SAD, a combination of drugs and cognitive therapy seems most effective. For bipolar depression, drug therapy is preferred.

Biological treatments

Drug therapy

Antidepressant drugs affect neurotransmitter levels. They include:

- **tricyclics**, which act to increase the activity of norepinephrine and serotonin
- **MAOIs** (monoamine oxidase inhibitors) which stop the breakdown of norepinephrine
- **SSRIs** (selective serotonin reuptake inhibitors) such as Prozac (fluoxetine), which prolong serotonin activity at the synapse

Evaluation

- Effectiveness rates: tricylics 60%, MAOIs 50% and SSRIs about 60% (Comer, 2008). SSRIs are fast-acting (around 2 weeks).

- Tricyclic side effects include dry mouth, perspiration, constipation and sexual dysfunction.

- MAOIs have serious side effects without a strict diet.

- Side effects of SSRIs include anxiety, agitation and reported increased risk of suicide.

- Not everyone responds to medication and it does not work immediately.

For bipolar disorder, **lithium** is used. It alters activity in the neuron and in doing so may restore levels of neurotransmitters to normal. It is most effective for mania. Dosage must be carefully monitored and there are unpleasant side effects (possible kidney dysfunction). Patients often stop taking lithium during the manic phase, leading to relapse.

Electroconvulsive therapy (ECT)
ECT induces a brain seizure by passing electricity through the brain. Anaesthetic and muscle relaxant are given, then electrodes are placed on the head (bilateral or unilateral) and an electric shock is given. The seizure usually lasts around a minute. A course of 6–12 sessions is typical. It is used with cases that do not respond to medication and is effective for 50% of people (Fink, 2001).
- The mode of action is not known.
- Side effects include memory loss, guilt and possible permanent damage.
- Relapse rates are high (80%) and further treatment is often required.

Light therapy (phototherapy)
This involves exposure to bright light during the winter months. It has been shown to alleviate SAD rapidly, especially if used in the morning (Eastman et al., 1998). Light therapy probably affects levels of melatonin, although the mechanism is unclear.

Cognitive treatments
Rational emotive therapy (RET)
RET attempts to replace irrational thoughts with rational ones. The therapist challenges irrational beliefs through confrontation and argument.

Cognitive behaviour therapy (CBT)
CBT focuses on changing the cognitive triad in four phases:
  (1) increasing confidence and elevating mood
  (2) challenging automatic negative thoughts
  (3) identifying biased thinking
  (4) changing attitudes and beliefs

Beck's therapy involves 'the patient as scientist'. The patient sets hypotheses to test negative beliefs and gathers evidence to challenge them. Between sessions a diary is used to monitor thoughts.

> **Study: Hollon et al. (2006)**
> Hollon et al. compared the effectiveness of cognitive therapy and drug therapy for depression. Over 16 weeks, patients received drug therapy or cognitive therapy. After 1 year, approximately 40% of the cognitive therapy group had relapsed, compared to 45% of the drug therapy group. A placebo group showed around 80% relapse.

- Cognitive therapy is effective, especially when combined with drug therapy.

- Cognitive therapy is not helpful in the manic phase of bipolar depression.

- Patients need to be reasonably articulate and well motivated.

Stress and stress management

Stress and illness

Summary specification content

The role of the automatic nervous system (ANS) and endocrine system functions in mediating and responding to stress.

Ways of measuring stress, including physiological, behavioural and self-report techniques.

The role of personal variables, including behaviour types A, B and C, locus of control and hardiness in mediating responses to stress.

Stress has been linked to illness (Kimvaki et al., 2002). People under stress also behave unhealthily, for example they have a poor diet and drink more alcohol, which may increase risk of illness (Ng and Jeffery, 2003). Johnson (2002) distinguished between chronic stress (over a sustained period) and acute stress (over a short period). Chronic stress affects the autonomic nervous system.

> ### Study: Cohen et al. (1991)
> Cohen et al. exposed participants to the cold virus. They also completed a stress questionnaire and were classified as high or low stress. In the high stress group, 47% developed a cold compared to only 27% in the low stress group.

The role of the autonomic nervous system (ANS)

The ANS is a section of the nervous system responsible for autonomic (involuntary) functions. It is comprised of sympathetic and parasympathetic sections. The sympathetic section prepares the body for action (flight or fight) by increasing heart rate. The parasympathetic section restores body functioning back to normal.

The role of the endocrine system

The endocrine system is made up of glands that secrete hormones into the bloodstream. Once in the bloodstream, these hormones continue to have an effect for a number of hours. The pituitary gland and adrenal gland are involved in the body's response to stress.

When a stressor is perceived, the sympathetic section of the ANS is activated: the adrenal medulla releases **adrenaline** and noradrenaline, increasing heart rate and blood flow. Meanwhile the hypothalamus produces corticotropin-releasing factor (CRF), stimulating the pituitary gland to secrete adrenocorticotrophic hormone (ACTH). This enters the circulation and stimulates the adrenal cortex to produce corticosteroids (including the hormone cortisol), which control glucose metabolism. These fight inflammation but can weaken the immune system causing illness over a sustained stressful period (Vedhara et al., 1999).

Long-term exposure to stress and continued bodily arousal is damaging; prolonged cardiovascular reactivity can cause strokes (Dougall and Baum, 2001). Schnall et al. (1990) found enlarged hearts in people with stressful jobs and Patterson et al. (1995) found increased blood cholesterol.

Study: Willis et al. (1987)

Willis et al. studied cortisol levels over time. Participants contacted the researchers when they experienced a stressful incident. Levels were measured at the time and afterwards. Cortisol was raised at the time of the incident and lower afterwards.

Evaluation

- Explaining stress purely in physiological terms is reductionist. Experience and feelings are also important.

- Some moderate or brief stress can be beneficial (eustress), stimulating the cardio-vascular and respiratory systems.

Ways of measuring stress

Physiological techniques

Hormone levels (corticosteroids and catecholamines) can be determined using blood and urine samples. Blood pressure, heart rate, rate of breathing and galvanic skin responses (GSR) can be measured. The GSR measures the skin's surface moisture by assessing the level of conductivity. Polygraphs allow for a number of physiological measures at the same time. A baseline is established before there is exposure to a stressor. Physiological changes are recorded.

Evaluation

- Physiological measures are objective.

- Arousal is not the same as stress. Other factors create arousal, e.g. humour.

- Special equipment and training are required.

- The measures themselves may be stressful.

- Variables such as weight and exercise can affect the results.

Behavioural techniques

Everyday behaviours can be measured (e.g. rate of speech) or more controlled measures may be taken by in a laboratory. Typical laboratory stressors are loud noise, overcrowding, electric shocks and extreme temperature. Behavioural stress measures include aggression (verbal or non-verbal) and speech measures such as stuttering.

> **Study: Glass and Singer (1972)**
> Glass and Singer exposed participants to loud noise while a control group worked in the quiet. The control group performed better on problem-solving and proofreading tasks. The researchers concluded that noise stressors have a negative effect on cognitive tasks.

Evaluation

- Performance measures are objective.

- Exposure to unpleasant stressors may be unethical.

- Laboratory stress is artificial.

- Behavioural techniques measure the consequences of stress rather than stress.

Self-report techniques

Self-report measures involve people giving their perceived level of stress, reporting their stress-related behaviours or assessing their experience of stress/stress events. Rating scales and questionnaires are used, although some studies use interviews or diaries.

The Holmes and Rahe (1967) Social Readjustment Rating Scale (SRRS) is a question-naire about stressful life events occurring in the previous year. Each event has a score. A high score on the SRRS means a person is highly stressed and vulnerable to stress-related illness.

Evaluation

- The SRRS is crude and neglects individual differences.

- Giving a single score is an oversimplification.

- A stressful event can be negative for one person and positive for another (e.g. divorce).

- Many SRRS events occur only rarely. A better everyday measure may be the Hassles and Uplifts scale (Kanner et al., 1981), which focuses on small everyday hassles.

Peacock and Wong's (1990) Stress Appraisal Measure (SAM) is another self-report measure. It measures stress (real or potential) by scoring events for potential harm (threat), challenge and perceived importance.

Evaluation

- Questionnaires and ratings are quick and easy to administer.

- Self-report measures require insight, which people do not always have.

- The measures are subjective.

- The measures do not tell us about physiological reactions to stress.

The role of personal variables in mediating responses to stress

Type A, B and C behaviours

Friedman and Rosenman (1974) identified a personality type that is more likely to respond negatively to stress: the type A personality. Friedman and Rosenman (1959) suggested type A people were more at risk of heart disease than type Bs. More recent research has focused on one aspect of type A (anger and hostility) in coronary heart disease (Kop and Krantz, 1997).

Type A people show the following characteristics: competitiveness and achievement orientation, time urgency, anger and hostility.

Type B people show the opposite traits and are easy going: low competitiveness, low time urgency, friendly and positive.

> ### Study: Friedman and Rosenman (1959)
> Friedman and Rosenman interviewed men about work, exercise, diet etc. Their cholesterol levels and heart function were also measured. Using colleague assessments, the men were identified as type A or type B. Type A men were more likely than type Bs to be at risk of heart disease. They worked longer hours and had a family history of heart disease.

Type C has recently been identified and has been linked to susceptibility to cancer. Type C people are passive, uncomplaining and compliant. Holland and Lewis (1996) argue that emotional suppression may lead to illness. Cohen and Herbert (1996) have linked type C with depression.

Evaluation

- Assessment usually involves interviews and behavioural observation so the outcome has some reliability.

- Hostility may be more important than other elements of type A.

- Myrtek (2001) argued that type A could not usefully predict heart disease.

- Type B and type C show some overlap.

Locus of control

Locus of control is a person's perceived control over what happens to them (Rotter, 1966). People with an internal locus of control believe they are in control of events in their life. High (not extreme) internal control is associated with less physical and psychological illness. Those with external locus believe they are not in control of what happens to them and extreme external locus can lead to helplessness, stress and depression. An extreme internal locus can also cause stress because it is impossible to control all events in our life. A balanced locus of control leads to low stress.

Study: Frankenhauser (1975)

Frankenhauser studied workers in a monotonous and dull job at a saw mill, measuring catecholamine levels, blood pressure, reported headaches and stomach problems. The workers showed high stress levels on all measures due to their lack of control over their boring work.

Evaluation

- Locus of control is assessed by the self-report locus of control scale and is therefore subjective.

- People may have perceived control in some areas of life and not others. The original measure was a global measure.

Hardiness

Kobasa (1979) identified hardiness as three traits that together appear to help resist the effects of stress:

- **commitment** (to family, job, community etc.)
- seeing events as a **challenge** or opportunity rather than an threat
- **control** (autonomy over own life)

Hardy people have a sense of purpose. They feel in control and thrive on challenge, perceiving stressful events positively.

Study: Kobasa et al. (1982)

Kobasa et al. assessed a large sample of US executives for hardiness. They were also measured for stressful life experiences and illness. Those with high hardiness scores had less illness than those with low hardiness scores, even though their level of exposure to stress was the same.

Evaluation

- Even hardy people are eventually worn down by stress (burn out) (Rowe, 1997).

- Most research uses self-reporting and is therefore subjective.

- Hardiness may apply to men rather than women.

Stress management

Summary specification content

Problem-focused and emotion-focused strategies. The role of defence mechanisms in coping with stress, including repression, regression, rationalisation and denial.

Techniques of stress management: behavioural approaches, including biofeedback and systematic desensitisation; cognitive therapy.

The role of social factors in coping with stress: social support, including types of social support.

Lazarus (1993) proposed a two-stage model of stress appraisal. The **transactional model** explains how stress results from interaction between the event and how the person appraises the event. In primary appraisal, the person considers whether the event is potentially stressful. In secondary appraisal, the person decides whether he or she has the ability to cope (self-efficacy). Lazarus distinguishes between three types of stress: loss, threat and challenge. Challenge can be both positive and negative.

Problem-focused and emotion-focused strategies

Lazarus (1999) suggested strategies can be:
- **problem-focused** — addressing the problem or event causing the stress
- **emotion-focused** — addressing the emotional reaction to stress

Folkman (1986) identified eight coping strategies.

Problem-focused strategies include:
- planful problem-solving — developing and executing a plan to deal with the stressor
- confronting — tackling the problem 'head on', which need not be aggressive

Emotion-focused strategies include:
- distancing — putting the problem at a distance, e.g. through humour
- positive reappraisal — seeing the positive side of the situation, 'looking on the bright side'

Study: Billings and Moos (1981)

Billings and Moos asked married couples about how they coped with a recent crisis. Males and females tended to use more problem-focused than emotion-focused strategies. However, women used more emotion-focused strategies than men. All preferred emotion-focused strategies for personal loss (e.g. death).

Evaluation

- Different stressors require different strategies.
- Strategies are often used in combination.
- Research focuses on identification of strategies rather than effectiveness.
- Individuals differ in their ability to use strategies. Nolen-Hoeksema et al. (1997) point out that 'ruminators' who dwell on problems are less likely to address the issue.

The role of defence mechanisms

According to the psychodynamic approach, unconscious defence mechanisms help us to cope with unpleasant stressful events and thoughts. They are emotion-focused strategies in that they do not address the problem directly. Instead, they reduce the emotional response. They include repression, regression, rationalisation and denial.
- **Repression** involves unconsciously pushing memories of an unpleasant stressful event (e.g. an argument) from conscious awareness. Freud believed that repressed memories may manifest themselves as anxiety disorders at some later time.

- **Regression** involves reverting to childlike behaviour (e.g. having a temper tantrum) to relieve the experience of stress.
- **Rationalisation** involves explaining an unpleasant stressful event in positive terms (e.g. being sacked is good because you can get a better job).
- **Denial** involves refusing to acknowledge that an unpleasant stressful event is happening (e.g. a man does not accept his wife has left him). Denial helps in the short term, giving time to adjust, but the problem may persist or worsen.

Evaluation

■ Most defence mechanisms help in the short term only.

■ In the long term, they may be damaging.

■ Some defence mechanisms, such as intellectualisation, can be productive in the long term.

■ Defence mechanisms are unconscious so cannot be studied.

Techniques of stress management

Behavioural approaches
Behavioural approaches aim to change behaviour to help reduce stress.

Biofeedback
Biofeedback is based on operant conditioning principles. Physiological functions (e.g. heart rate) are monitored and feedback (visual or auditory) is given. As the physiological functions fluctuate (e.g. heart rate slows minutely), positive reinforcement is given. This may simply be seeing the lower readout on the monitor. The person can then work to try to reduce the heart rate further and receive more reinforcement. Training is laboratory-based. Thermal biofeedback is sometimes used for stress because skin temperature is low when stressed.

Study: Scharff et al. (2002)
Scharff et al. trained children who suffered stress migraines in hand-warming biofeedback. There were two other groups: a hand-cooling group and a control group. The hand-warming group reported fewer migraines than other groups for up to 6 months.

Evaluation

■ Biofeedback is effective for anxiety and headaches (Gatchel et al., 1989).

■ Biofeedback may be no better than simple relaxation (Lehrer et al., 1994).

■ It is expensive in relation to other techniques.

■ There may be a placebo effect.

■ The technique is difficult to use in real-life situations.

Systematic desensitisation

Systematic desensitisation involves the gradual systematic exposure to a stressor. Graded exposure to a stimulus hierarchy is combined with relaxation techniques to help the person deal the stressful stimulus. The technique is based on classical conditioning principles, counter-conditioning the person to feel calm.

Study: Morrow et al. (1992)

Morrow et al. studied systematic desensitisation with cancer patients receiving chemotherapy. The systematic desensitisation group was compared with a control group for duration of nausea after chemotherapy. On average the control group experienced 15 hours more nausea than the treatment group. The treatment reduced the stress of chemotherapy and the side effects.

Evaluation

- Systematic desensitisation can be effective.

- It cannot help where stress is unexpected.

- It treats the response to stress rather than the cause.

Cognitive therapy

Cognitive therapy involves cognitive restructuring to replace negative thoughts caused by stress.

Rational emotive therapy (RET)

This was proposed by Ellis (1962). Ellis said that people often have irrational beliefs that lead them to feel stressed (e.g. 'I must be loved and accepted by everyone I meet'). As a result, they catastrophise and feel stressed and unable to cope. RET helps the person replace irrational and catastrophic beliefs with rational, positive and realistic beliefs. RET involves rational confrontation where the therapist challenges the client's irrational beliefs through robust argument.

Stress inoculation training (SIT)

Meichenbaum (1996) proposed three stages of SIT:
  (1) conceptualisation (the stress is understood)
  (2) skills acquisition (skills to manage the stress are rehearsed, e.g. positive self-talk)
  (3) application (skills are applied)

SIT has been used with patients before surgery and to manage pain (Meichenbaum, 1996). Training is flexible, varying from a single, short session to hourly sessions over many weeks.

Study: Jaremko (2006)

Jaremko used SIT with students to control the stress of public speaking. Participants reported less anxiety (stress) after being trained in SIT.

- Cognitive and behavioural techniques can be successful in combination.

- Cognitive therapies recognise that stress often involves distorted thinking, which affects behaviour and emotion.

- Many people find RET too aggressive.

- RET techniques are most suitable for articulate and motivated clients.

- SIT is flexible and can be used with individuals, couples and small groups.

The role of social factors in coping with stress

Social support usually comes from friends, neighbours, family etc. It may buffer the effect of stress (Cohen and Wills, 1985). Cohen et al. (1986) found that social support is greater for people with good communication and social skills, presumably because they have more extensive social networks.

Stroebe (2000) noted five types of social support:
- **appraisal** support — others help the person understand the stressors
- **emotional** support — others show love/care
- **esteem** support — others help strengthen feelings of self-worth
- **informational** support — others give advice and guidance (this may be professional)
- **instrumental** support — others provide practical help

Study: Sosa et al. (1980)

Sosa et al. investigated the effects of instrumental support in childbirth. Women in one group received social support during labour. A control group had no extra social support. The social support group reported a better experience and had much shorter labours than the control group. Instrumental social support helped with the stress of labour.

Study: Berkman and Syme (1979)

Berkman and Syme followed a large sample over 9 years, recording social support using questionnaires on marital status, friends etc. They found that those with little social support were more likely to die during the study.

- Social support varies according to gender (women offer emotional support more than men) and culture (support from extended family is more common in traditional cultures).

- Too much social support can be overwhelming and add to stress.

- Social support is so varied it is difficult to assess the effectiveness.

- Social support is measured using self-report, which is subjective.

Substance abuse

Use and abuse

Summary specification content

Distinctions between addiction and physical dependence. Psychological dependence, tolerance and withdrawal. Solvent abuse, tobacco and nicotine, alcohol, stimulants and depressants.

Explanations for substance abuse: hereditary factors; personality characteristics and social factors, including peer influences.

Substance use is where taking a substance involves no harm. Substance abuse is where the substance harms either the person taking it or others. What is use and abuse varies in different societies.

Distinctions between addiction and physical dependence

Addiction occurs when, with repeated use, someone becomes preoccupied with a substance and dependent on it. The addictive behaviour causes a pleasant feeling (high). Increasing levels have to be taken to maintain the pleasant feeling. Withdrawal symptoms are experienced when the substance is not taken. Relationships with others suffer and the risk of relapse is high.

In **physical dependence**, the body has got used to the substance and needs it to be in a 'normal' state, i.e. without withdrawal symptoms. This is because drugs act by changing brain chemistry.

Psychological dependence

In **psychological dependence**, there is an emotional and mental compulsion to keep taking the substance. The drug becomes the focus of life and determines daily routines. There is craving — a motivational state of want and desire — for the drug.

Pinel (2003) argues the distinction between physical and psychological dependence is not useful as both are involved in addiction.

Tolerance

Tolerance occurs when the body adapts to the substance over time and so more is required to have the same physical and psychological effects. The same amount creates less effect than when it was first used and more is needed to produce a similar effect. Some drugs, such as cannabis, do not result in tolerance.

Siegel et al.'s (1982) theory of conditioned drug tolerance explains how the same level of drug usage, but in different settings, can result in drug overdose.

Study: Siegel et al. (1982)

Siegel et al. gave rats heroin in their usual environment for 80 days. Half the rats were then put in a different environment and the other half remained in the usual place. All rats were then given a high dose of heroin. Many of those in the new environment died of the overdose (65%), compared with only 30% in the usual environment.

Withdrawal

Withdrawal is the unpleasant physical and psychological side effects experienced when use of a drug is suddenly stopped. Withdrawal occurs if a drug has been used for some time and tolerance has developed. The effects are usually the opposite of the pleasant effects of a drug. Symptoms are unpleasant so relapse is likely, especially in a time of stress. Withdrawal requires careful management.

- Nicotine withdrawal symptoms include cravings, depression, sleep problems, irritability and increased appetite.
- Alcohol withdrawal symptoms include sweating, anxiety, nausea, tremors and cramps.
- Heroin withdrawal symptoms include anxiety, pain, diarrhoea, shivering and sweating.

Solvent abuse

Solvents include glue, paint, nail varnish and removers, aerosols and lighter fuel. At room temperature they evaporate and the fumes can be inhaled. The effect is similar to that of alcohol. A fifth of 15–16-year-olds say they have used solvents (Drugscope, 2001). Solvents are toxic and can cause brain damage and lung disorders.

Study: Field-Smith et al. (2002)

Field-Smith et al. studied UK data from 1971 to 2000. They found that between 1990 and 2000, the solvent abuse death rate fell from 152 to 64. They also found that 80% of deaths involved males.

Tobacco and nicotine

Tobacco contains nicotine, a mild **stimulant**. Nicotine enters the bloodstream rapidly and levels decline rapidly. This means that someone must smoke regularly to keep the nicotine at a certain level. Tomkins (1968) distinguished between habitual smokers who smoke out of habit without much awareness and addictive smokers who are aware of when they are and are not smoking.

Factors that explain why people start to smoke include peer pressure, role models, parents and friends smoking, rebelliousness and risk-taking personality.

Robinson and Klesges (1997) found teenagers think smoking projects a grown-up image. One biological explanation is the **nicotine regulation model**.

Study: Schachter et al. (1977)

Schachter et al. asked smokers to smoke low-nicotine cigarettes for one week and high-nicotine cigarettes for the next week. Participants smoked more low-nicotine than high-nicotine cigarettes. It seems that smokers try to maintain a certain nicotine level in the body, supporting the biological nicotine regulation model.

Alcohol

Alcohol is absorbed quickly into the bloodstream. It is addictive and leads to tolerance if it is drunk every day. It causes physical and psychological dependence. The recommended weekly limits are 21 units for men and 14 units for women. Negative effects of heavy drinking on health include liver disease and amnesia (Korsakoff's syndrome). Alcohol use has been linked to aggression and antisocial personality (Zucker et al., 1996).

Stimulants

These stimulate the central nervous system, causing euphoria and energy. They include amphetamines (e.g. ecstasy), cocaine and alkyl nitrites ('poppers'). Amphetamines increase heart rate and blood supply to the muscles and increase dopamine levels in the brain. Tolerance develops quickly. Withdrawal symptoms include exhaustion and depression. Ecstasy is a hallucinogenic amphetamine. Animal studies show it can damage nerve cells. Cocaine has immediate but short-lived effects of wellbeing and confidence. Tolerance does not develop and withdrawal effects are not severe in comparison to alcohol and heroin. Alkyl nitrites dilate the blood vessels and are meant to enhance sexual performance. They are not illegal. After-effects include headaches and nausea.

Depressants

Depressants induce calmness by slowing down central nervous system activity. High doses of depressants can cause unconsciousness. Alcohol and solvents are depressants. Others include **opiates** (e.g. heroin), **tranquillisers** (e.g. diazepam) and **barbiturates** (sleeping pills). Heroin (a Class A drug) can be injected or smoked and is thought to be highly addictive. It results in euphoria but a tolerance soon develops. Tranquillisers (Class B drugs) are prescribed for anxiety disorders. They act to release GABA, a neuro-transmitter, which results in calmness and sleep. They are usually prescribed for short-term use as tolerance and dependence develop easily. Withdrawal symptoms include insomnia, sweating, tremors, loss of appetite and irritability.

Explanations for substance abuse
Hereditary factors

A predisposition to alcohol abuse may be genetic. Melo et al. (1996) selectively bred animals that preferred alcohol with one another. The offspring were found to prefer alcohol to other drinks. Human twin research suggests there may be a predisposition to substance abuse and dependence.

Study: Kaij (1960)

Kaij studied alcohol abuse in identical (MZ) twins and non-identical (DZ) twins. The concordance rate was 54% in MZ pairs and 28% in DZ pairs. This result supports the genetic explanation for alcohol abuse.

Evaluation

- Even MZ pairs are not 100% concordant.

- Higher MZ than DZ rates would also be predicted by environmentalists as MZ pairs have a more shared environment than DZ pairs.

- Twin studies often use small samples and can be unreliable (in early studies MZ or DZ status was not always clear).

Adoption studies compare adopted children with their biological parents. Adoptees who abused alcohol as adults were likely to have a biological parent who abused alcohol (Goldstein, 1994). Peters and Preedy (2002) reported that 18% of adoptees with a biological parent who abused alcohol became alcohol abusers compared to 5% of adoptees in a control group. One large-scale adoption study by Cloninger (1987) showed that approximately 17% of sons of alcohol-abusing fathers became alcohol abusers, as opposed to approximately 3% of controls.

Gene mapping techniques have found abnormal dopamine-linked genes in 60% of alcohol abusers and 50% of people who use cocaine regularly (Melo et al., 1996).

Evaluation

- Biological explanations are reductionist and oversimplified.

- There may be a genetic influence, but social factors are also important.

- Plomin (1990) argues for a genetic effect in the form of an absence of a control mechanism.

Personality characteristics

Substance abuse may be related to personality. Flory et al. (2002) found alcohol abuse was more common in extroverts. McAdams (2000) linked alcohol abuse with low levels of conscientiousness. According to psychodynamic theory, substance abusers have strong levels of dependency linked to early childhood (Shedler and Block, 1990). A child whose needs are not satisfied by parents may become over-dependent as an adult and use drugs as substitute comfort. Antisocial personality disorder (APD) has been found to be associated with several forms of substance abuse (Fabrega et al., 1991).

Study: Morgenstern et al. (1997)

Morgenstern et al. used interviews to establish personality characteristics and patterns of alcohol abuse with abusers attending a treatment centre. Traits typical of APD were found to be associated with alcohol abuse.

Evaluation

- Various traits are linked to abuse and some evidence is contradictory.

- Establishing cause and effect is impossible in correlation studies.

- Most personality research is restricted to alcohol abuse.

Social factors and peer influences

Social learning, role models, peers, social norms and sociocultural factors may be involved in substance abuse. Social learning occurs through observation, imitation, modelling and vicarious reinforcement (learning through the consequences of behaviour for others). We are more likely to imitate models that are similar (e.g. in age) and high status (e.g. celebrities). For alcohol abuse, role models tend to be parents; for cannabis and cocaine abuse, role models are usually peers (Stein et al., 1987).

> **Study: Garnier and Stein (2002)**
>
> Garnier and Stein conducted a longitudinal study from when mothers were pregnant until 18 years later when their children were teenagers. Substance abuse in teenagers was significantly associated with substance abuse by peers.

The relationship between peer influence and behaviour is complicated because peer groups are part of a wider subculture with its own norms and values.

Norms of acceptable behaviour differ across cultures and subcultures, for example levels of alcohol abuse are linked to whether or not drunkenness is socially acceptable (Helzer and Canino, 1992).

Evaluation

■ High self-efficacy can reduce social and peer influences (Bandura, 1997).

■ Although drug use may be due to social influences, drug abuse may be more related to personal factors (e.g. genetics, personality).

Treatment and prevention

Summary specification content

Psychological treatments and their effectiveness, including aversion therapy and self-management.

Prevention techniques. Identifying and targeting 'risk' groups. Use of fear-arousing appeals. Social inoculation.

Health promotion/education in treatment and prevention. Stages of behaviour change proposed in the Prochaska model.

Psychological treatments and their effectiveness

Aversion therapy

Aversion therapy is based on classical conditioning. An abused substance is paired with an unpleasant stimulus (e.g. electric shock or emetic). After several pairings, the person becomes classically conditioned to fear or avoid the substance. Rapid smoking is a form of aversion therapy used to stop people smoking (Danaher, 1977). Forced rapid smoking is unpleasant and can effectively treat smoking, but it can be dangerous. **Covert sensitisation** therapy is a form of aversion therapy involving the association of unpleasant thoughts or images with the substance. Covert sensitisation seems to be effective for alcohol abuse and in helping to stop smoking (Emmelkamp, 1996).

> **Study: Wiens and Menustik (1983)**
>
> Wiens and Menustik treated a large sample of alcohol abusers with aversion therapy involving an emetic drug. Over 60% stopped drinking alcohol in the year after therapy and 30% remained alcohol-free for 2 years.

- Success with aversion therapy is limited and often short-term.

- The person must be motivated and needs support to cope with withdrawal.

- It can be successfully combined with other therapies, e.g. biological therapy.

- Aversion might be seen as unethical, although people must give consent.

- It has been used most with alcohol abuse and smoking. Behavioural treatments based on operant conditioning (e.g. contingency training) may be more effective for other substances.

Study: Higgins et al. (1993)

Higgins et al. used contingency training to treat cocaine abusers. They received incentives (lottery tickets) if their urine sample indicated they had not taken cocaine. After a 6-month programme, 68% were drug-free for at least 8 weeks.

Self-management

Self-management is often group-based and supervised by a health professional. It involves monitoring intake and gaining insight into the causes and consequences of abuse. Alcoholics Anonymous (AA) is one example. Moos and Moos (2004) found regular AA attendance helped people to stop drinking. Self-management can be community-based, for example the North Australia Coast Study for smoking led to a 30% reduction over 3 years.

Study: Botvin et al. (2001)

Botvin et al. used a community programme in inner-city schools with a large sample of teenagers. Information included the negative effects of binge drinking. Binge drinking was reduced in the programme compared to a control group.

One successful self-management strategy is cognitive behaviour therapy such as **behavioural self-control training** (Miller et al., 1992). Alcohol abusers use a combination of insight and practical techniques to self-manage their problem, leading to 70% improvement. The approach has also been successful with people who abuse cannabis and cocaine (Carrol and Rounsaville, 1995).

- Many groups do not keep records, so evaluation is difficult.

- Programmes vary enormously. Structured self-management involving cognitive-behaviour therapy seems most successful.

- Better programmes incorporate help to resist peer pressure.

Prevention techniques

Primary prevention is about preventing substance abuse starting. Secondary prevention is aimed at those at risk. Tertiary prevention is focused on preventing those already abusing from developing further problems.

Identifying risk groups

Limited resources can be targeted on those most at risk. Naidoo and Wills (1998) identified three risk factors:

- psychosocial (e.g. unemployment, social isolation, poor housing)
- cultural (e.g. Gray et al. (2000) found a risk of alcohol abuse in Aboriginal Australians)
- biological (e.g. family history)

Drug Action Teams (DATs) combine the efforts of social services, the police, education services and health professionals to target young people at risk.

Study: Drummond (2002)

Drummond investigated the role of accident and emergency (A and E) health workers in targeting alcohol abusers. People identified through A and E were invited to attend an advice clinic. Approximately 50% attended and discussed their problem.

Evaluation

- It is important to consider social and cultural problems and not just to focus on the individual.
- Drugs workers should be sensitive to people's circumstances.
- Identification of high-risk groups requires coordination of services.

Fear-arousing appeals

Fear-arousing appeals involve the use of shocking messages or images to deter people from substance abuse. Janis and Hovland (1959) identified three key factors to be considered when using fear appeals:

- **source** factors (e.g. expertise, trustworthiness and status of the source)
- **message** factors (e.g. type of message — high or low fear)
- **audience** factors (e.g. intelligence, self-esteem)

Baumeister and Covington (1985) found the effects of a fear appeal are more long-term in people with high self-esteem. Research suggests shocking messages are not effective.

Study: Janis and Feshbach (1953)

Janis and Feshbach used high, medium and low fear appeals in lectures on tooth decay. Strong fear appeal caused most anxiety and was rated as most interesting but led to the least behaviour change. Low fear appeal caused least anxiety in the audience but resulted in greatest behaviour change.

Evaluation

- Flay (1985) found fear appeals were not particularly effective for smoking prevention.
- High fear messages may lead people to 'switch off'.
- Fear appeals are indiscriminate and not aimed at specific groups.
- Fear appeals compete with advertising campaigns which portray substances as desirable (Borum, 2000).

Social inoculation

Social inoculation involves training in resistance to persuasion and changing attitudes and behaviour. Flay et al. (1985) identified four key elements:

- **knowledge** about the negative effects
- **discussion** about the roles of **peers** etc.
- **skill development** to resist and deflect peer criticism
- **public commitment** to not take or abuse

Study: McAlister et al. (1980)

McAlister et al. used social inoculation techniques with teenagers. They learned and rehearsed arguments about why they should not smoke. Over a number of years they were less likely to smoke compared to a control group.

Evaluation

- Social inoculation helps people resist social pressure.

- Programmes are best delivered by someone similar to the target group or of high status.

- Cuijpers et al. (2002) found social inoculation in Dutch schools led to reduced alcohol use but increased cannabis use.

- Little research has been carried out with older people.

Health promotion/education in treatment and prevention

Health promotion uses four main methods:

- **information giving** (e.g. about medical conditions linked to substance abuse)
- **information to motivate** — to make the person to want to be healthy
- **motivational interviewing** — usually one-to-one
- **behavioural techniques** — to replace unhealthy behaviours with healthy ones

Campaigns can take place at school, at work or in the community.

Study: Moher et al. (2005)

Moher et al. reviewed the effectiveness of work-based attempts to help employees stop smoking. Some programmes focused on individuals (e.g. counselling, nicotine replacement). Others were aimed at the whole work force (e.g. bans, incentive schemes). Strategies aimed at individuals were more effective.

The Prochaska model of behaviour change

Prochaska et al. (1992) proposed a six-stage spiral model of behaviour change. The model acknowledges that people do not always succeed in changing their behaviour at first. Some go through some stages several times before success. The six stages are as follows:

(1) **pre-contemplation** — person is not aware of problem
(2) **contemplation** — person is aware of problem and has started to think about changing

(3) preparation — person has decided to change behaviour soon

(4) action — behaviour changes for at least 1 day

(5) maintenance — behaviour change is maintained for 6 months

(6) termination — new behaviour is now 'normal' and relapse is unlikely

Evaluation

- There is a high rate of success with programmes based on this model.

- The structure reduces a difficult task into manageable steps.

Forensic psychology

Offending behaviour

Summary specification content

Problems in defining crime. Measuring crime, including official statistics and alternatives (victim surveys and self-report measures). Offender profiling, including typology and geographical approaches.

Theories of offending. Physiological approaches: atavistic form and somatotype theories. Biological explanations, including genetic transmission. Psychodynamic and learning theory explanations, including social learning. Eysenck's theory of the criminal personality.

Problems in defining crime

Factors such as historical context, culture, age of offender and specific circumstances all make it difficult to define crime.

- When — what was once a crime may no longer be a crime and vice versa.
- Where — a crime in one culture may not be elsewhere.
- Who — in the UK the age of criminal responsibility is 10 years.
- What — some 'crimes' are committed with good rather than bad intent.

Measuring crime

Three ways of measuring crime are official statistics, victim surveys and offender self-reports.

Official statistics

These consist of **reported** and **recorded** crime. Hollin (1992) estimated these account for only 25% of crime. The 'dark figure' of crime is those offences that are not included in official statistics. Differences in police recording rules may affect recorded crime in different areas.

Study: Farrington and Dowds (1985)

Farrington and Dowds analysed records of crimes in Nottinghamshire and two neighbouring counties. They found Nottinghamshire police recorded crimes under £10 value whereas the other forces did not, distorting official figures.

Victim surveys

People are asked if they have been a crime victim, such as in the British Crime Survey (BCS), conducted biennially. The survey also collects data on attitudes to crime and fear of crime.

For the 2006 BCS a large sample of 16–24-year-olds was interviewed using a structured interview. The BCS results showed an overall crime increase of 3% compared to official figures, which showed an overall decrease of 2%.

Self-report measures

These involve asking offenders to report their offending behaviour. Self-report surveys focus on people previously convicted and other groups known to be at risk of offending.

The Offending, Crime and Justice Survey (OCJS) involves interviewing 10–25-year-olds about antisocial behaviour (e.g. shoplifting) and drug use. It is a longitudinal study as the same people are interviewed over time. The 2006 survey showed that alcohol was a key factor in offending.

Evaluation

- The 'dark figure' of crime is neglected in official statistics.

- Victim survey data is based on retrospective reporting.

- Offender self-reporting assumes honesty.

Offender profiling

Offender profiling is used to predict personality or behavioural characteristics of an offender based on analysis of the crime. Initially used by the FBI, it allows investigators to narrow down the field of possible suspects.

The typology approach

Interviews with 36 sex offenders in the USA led to a belief that sexually motivated murderers and some arsonists could be classified as **organised** or **disorganised** offenders (Douglas et al., 1992). Organised offenders plan the offence, target a stranger and leave little evidence. They tend to be socially competent, in a skilled job and living with a partner. Disorganised offenders do not plan, know the victim and leave evidence. They tend to be socially inadequate, unskilled and living alone.

Study: Canter et al. (2004)

Canter et al. analysed data from 100 murders for characteristics typical of either organised or disorganised offenders. They found evidence for the existence of a subset of organised characteristics in most serial killers, but concluded that no subset of disorganised characteristics existed and therefore the disorganised type had no validity.

Evaluation

- The validity of the US typology has been questioned.

- The distinction is based on a small sample.

- A third category 'mixed' offender was added later.

- Modern personality theory suggests behaviour is not consistent across different situations, conflicting with the idea of a typology (Alison et al., 2002).

Geographical approaches

Geographical approaches involve inferring the offender's base on the basis of crime locations (Rossmo, 1997) and assume that offenders like to operate in familiar areas. Canter and Gregory (1994) found many offenders have a crime range of only 2 miles. Geographical profiling is based on schema theory about the mental representation of information. An offender's mental map determines where his or her crimes are committed and knowledge of this enables investigators to predict the offender's base and typical everyday movements, narrowing down the search area.

Study: Canter (1986)

Canter profiled the Railway Rapist (John Duffy), who was responsible for sexual assaults and murders in London. Using geographical information and witness reports, Canter's remarkably accurate profile led to Duffy's arrest. The profile correctly predicted where Duffy lived, that he was separated and worked on the railways.

Study: Lundrigan and Canter (2001)

Lundrigan and Canter used information from solved murder cases, analysing distances between the offender's home and body disposal locations. They found that the offender's home was often geographically central to disposal sites and that disposal often followed a predictable pattern.

Evaluation

- Geographical approaches are based on memory theory (schema theory).

- They can be used for different types of crimes, including burglary.

- Geographical information alone is insufficient. Other information such as crime scene behaviour, timing and nature of the victim are also relevant.

Evaluation of offender profiling

- Profiles contribute to identification in few cases (Pinizzotto, 1984).

- 70% of police officers questioned its usefulness (Bartol, 1996).

- Pinizzotto and Finkel (1990) tested five groups on their ability to construct profiles for a previously solved murder and sex offence. Trained profilers produced more accurate profiles for the sex case but not for the murder.

Theories of offending

Physiological approaches

Lombroso's atavistic form

Lombroso (1876) argued that offenders were a separate species, a primitive genetic form (**atavistic**). He noted that convicts had distinctive **physical anomalies** (e.g. large jaws, extra hair) and proposed that they were born criminals.

Sheldon's somatotype theory

Sheldon (1949) proposed three different body shapes or constitutions: endomorphs, ectomorphs and mesomorphs. He suggested that the muscular **mesomorph** was the criminal constitution, showing aggressive traits.

> **Study: Sheldon (1949)**
> Sheldon rated photographs of delinquents and controls on a scale of 1–7 for mesomorphy. The average rating was 4.6 for the delinquent photos and 3.8 for the controls.

Evaluation

- Goring (1913) found little evidence of atavistic features in a large sample.

- Criminality became associated with ethnic groups possessing atavistic-type features.

- The idea of a criminal stereotype is rooted in Lombroso's theory.

- Sheldon did not use the legal criteria for delinquency and rated the photographs himself.

- People with certain features and build may be expected to be aggressive, leading to a self-fulfilling prophecy.

Biological explanations

Genetics

An early study of criminal concordance by Lange (1929) found identical (MZ) twin rates of 77% and non-identical (DZ) twin rates of 12%, suggesting criminality is inherited.

> **Study: Grove et al. (1990)**
> Grove et al. investigated concordance in MZ pairs separated soon after birth. Each was interviewed in adulthood and scored for psychiatric disorder and antisocial personality. The rate of concordance for antisocial personality disorder was 29%, suggesting that antisocial traits were partly genetic.

> ### Study: Mednick et al. (1984)
> Mednick et al. studied adopted children in Denmark, comparing their criminal conviction rates with those of their biological and adoptive parents. Of those with criminal biological parents, 20% had convictions. The rate was 13.5% in those with no biological history of criminality.

Chromosomes

Criminality was once linked to the atypical sex chromosome pattern, **XYY** (Jacobs et al., 1965). However, Witkin et al. (1976) found very few cases of XYY in a huge sample and this theory of offending is no longer accepted.

Neurophysiology

Certain brain structures (limbic system and amygdala) control aggression in animals. People with antisocial personality disorder (APD) show abnormal EEG patterns, indicating brain immaturity which may explain impulsive, self-centred behaviour.

> ### Study: Raine et al. (2000)
> Raine et al. used scans to measure brain volume in people with APD and controls. An 11% reduction in grey matter was noted in the prefrontal area for APD participants.

Evaluation

- Even MZ pairs are not 100% concordant.
- Early twin studies were unreliable (e.g. they were not always properly determined as MZ or DZ, not always separated).
- Criminal behaviour of biological parent and child may be due to inherited mental disorder rather than inherited criminality.
- Biological explanations are reductionist and oversimplified.

Psychodynamic explanations

Superego

The **superego** is internalised through identification with the same-sex parent in the phallic stage. It is the internal parent or conscience. Blackburn (1993) suggested offending may be due to:

- a **weak superego** (the child has not identified and has no moral code)
- a **deviant superego** (the child identifies with an immoral parent)
- an **over-harsh superego** (the child misbehaves to fulfil an unconscious desire for punishment and guilt)

Maternal deprivation

Bowlby (1951) used evidence from animal studies and his study of 44 juvenile delinquents to propose that maternal deprivation in the first 2 years may lead to delinquency and affectionless behaviour.

Defence mechanisms

These protect the conscious self from unpleasant thoughts and ideas. Defence mechanisms can explain crime in various ways, for example an offender may use **denial** (refusing to consciously acknowledge the seriousness of a crime) or **sublimation** may be used where an offender carries out a lesser (less unacceptable) crime instead of a more serious one.

Evaluation

- Unconscious processes cannot be tested empirically.

- Most people who grow up without a same-sex parent do not offend.

- Bowlby's research was retrospective and the theory much criticised.

Learning theory explanations

Behaviourists believe that criminal behaviour is learnt through association. Social learning theory (SLT, Bandura, 1977) predicted that offending is learnt through observation, imitation and vicarious reinforcement (learning through seeing the consequences for others). Sutherland (1939) proposed **differential association theory**. He suggested offending is learnt through association with peers, family etc. whose values we adopt. Sutherland argued that if offenders receive reinforcement (approval) from others for criminal behaviour, the behaviour will be repeated.

Study: Farrington (2006)

In a longitudinal study of boys in a deprived area, Farrington recorded details of background, parenting and criminal convictions. Over 40 years, 41% of participants had criminal convictions. Criminal family history and poor parenting were key factors, supporting learning theory explanations

Evaluation

- Learning explanations contrast directly with biological explanations.

- Poor socialisation is linked to crime but may not be the cause.

- Family history may support biological rather than social explanations.

Eysenck's theory of the criminal personality

Eysenck (1964) suggested our inherited nervous system dictates our personality and that people vary across two principal dimensions: introvert-extravert (IE) and neurotic-stable (NS). He later added a **psychoticism** (P) dimension (cold, heartless). Eysenck suggested that the criminal type is the **neurotic-extravert**. Extraverts have a chronically under-aroused nervous system which leads them to seek sensation; they are not easy to condition so cannot learn from mistakes. Neurotics are emotionally unstable and unpredictable.

Study: McGurk and McDougall (1981)

McGurk and McDougall compared Eysenck's Personality Inventory (EPI) scores for delinquents and non-delinquents. They found the delinquent group showed higher P, E and N scores than the controls.

Evaluation

■ Not all research indicates high E scores in delinquent populations.

■ More recent personality theories suggest other traits may be important.

■ Moffitt (1993) suggests there are different types of offenders, not just one.

■ The theory is testable and the EPI has good reliability.

Treatment of offenders

Summary specification content

The role of custodial sentencing. Effectiveness of custodial sentencing, including recidivism. Alternatives to custodial sentencing.

Treatment programmes: behaviour modification; social skills training and anger management.

Evaluation of these treatment programmes.

The role and effectiveness of custodial sentencing

A custodial sentence is a prison sentence. The aims of custodial sentencing are:

- **incapacitation** — offending cannot continue while in prison
- **rehabilitation** — reform of the offender into a better person
- **retribution** — society 'gets its own back'
- **deterrence** — putting the offender (and others) off committing further crime

Study: Zimbardo et al. (1973)

Zimbardo et al. studied the effects of imprisonment in a role-play experiment. Student volunteers were randomly allocated to roles of 'prisoner' or 'guard' in a role play to last 14 days. 'Prisoners' quickly became passive and submissive. 'Guards' abused their power, subjecting 'prisoners' to punishments. The research was stopped after 6 days because of prisoner anxiety and distress.

Evaluation

■ Davies and Raymond (2000) concluded that custodial sentences primarily serve the purpose of retribution.

■ Recidivism (re-offending) rates of approximately 75% in young males suggest custodial sentences do not reform or deter (Cullen and Minchin, 2000).

■ Prison has many negative effects including institutionalisation, psychological disturbance, brutalisation, loss of family contact and lowered employment prospects.

Alternatives to custodial sentencing

You need to be able to describe and evaluate two alternatives to custodial sentencing, such as antisocial behaviour orders, electronic tagging, community service or restorative justice.

Electronic tagging

Electronic tagging involves fixing an electronic device to an offender's ankle, enabling continuous monitoring of his or her movements and reducing the chance of further offending. Tagging can aid in the supervision of curfew orders where the court says an offender must remain at home during certain hours (usually during the evening). The tagging system was introduced in 1999.

Study: Cassidy et al. (2005)

Cassidy et al. studied juvenile offenders aged 12–16 years. They found tagging was used mostly with repeat offenders and that young males and black males were over-represented in the population. Tagging was found to lead to a 7% decrease in breach of bail conditions. The researchers concluded that tagging can be effective.

Evaluation

- Electronic tagging is cheap compared to custodial sentencing.
- It can be an effective alternative to custodial sentencing in helping prevent offending.
- Offenders can maintain family ties.
- The negative effects of prison can be avoided.

Restorative justice

This usually involves meetings between offender and victim, allowing the offender the opportunity to make amends and see the suffering the crime has caused. Restorative justice emphasises **psychological healing** and **collaboration**. It can also involve practical **reparation** (an offender giving something back in practical terms). It can be used alongside other forms of sentencing or on its own.

Study: Sherman and Strang (2007)

Sherman and Strang analysed studies comparing restorative justice and conventional punishments. Programmes varied but included victim–offender meetings and financial restitution. They found restorative justice resulted in reduced recidivism. For victims, desire for revenge and stress were reduced.

Evaluation

- Victims often do not want to meet the offender.
- Restorative justice can be seen as an easy option.
- Programmes vary so much that evaluation is difficult.
- Drop-out rates tend to be high.

Treatment programmes

Behaviour modification

Behaviour modification involves reinforcing desirable behaviour and extinguishing undesirable behaviour using **operant conditioning**. In prison this normally involves a **token economy** with tokens for good behaviour. These can then be exchanged for primary reinforcers such as food and videos.

Study: Cullen and Seddon (1981)

Cullen and Seddon used a token economy in a youth offenders' institution. Positive behaviours were rewarded and undesirable behaviours were not. Those taking part demonstrated more positive behaviours during the study.

Evaluation

- Token economies have ethical problems.

- They may lead to 'token learning' (superficial). Blackburn (1993) argued there is no real change.

- Benefits are mostly short-term, although Cohen and Filipczak (1971) found that recidivism was reduced for at least 2 years.

Social skills training

Social skills training involves training in skills at the micro level (e.g. eye contact) and the macro level (e.g. staring a conversation). It is based on observation, modelling of role models in role play, reinforcement/feedback and homework practice tasks.

Study: Long and Sherer (1985)

Long and Sherer compared a social skills training group, a group discussion group and a control group. Social skills training was most successful with the more regular offenders and group discussion was most successful with less regular offenders, both after training and in a follow-up review.

Evaluation

- Poor social skills may not cause offending.

- Perhaps improvements in social skills increase the ability to resist peer influences.

- Social skills training is no more effective than other group-based methods (Sarason, 1978).

- The effects are short term (Goldstein, 1986).

Anger management

Anger management programmes focus on understanding and controlling anger. Novaco (1985) identified three stages:

(1) cognitive preparation — the offender learns to recognise anger and situations that cause anger
(2) skill acquisition — techniques to control anger are taught, e.g. relaxation and self-talk
(3) application practice — new techniques are practised, e.g. in role play

Study: Ireland (2000)

Ireland studied group anger management over 12 hour-long sessions. Anger levels were assessed before and after the programme period. In the programme group, 92% showed improved anger levels on at least one measure. The researchers concluded the programme was effective.

Evaluation

- Anger management programmes are effective in the short term and make prisoners more manageable.

- They focus on changing understanding not just behaviour.

- Anger may not be the cause of offending (Loza and Loza-Fanous, 1999).

- Offenders must be motivated to change.

Questions
&
Answers

In this section of the guide, there are eight questions, one on each topic. Each question is worth 20 marks. You should allow 40 minutes when answering each question.

This section is structured as follows:
- sample questions in the style in which they appear on the Unit 3 examination paper
- analysis of each question, explaining what is expected in each sub-section of the question
- example candidate responses at the C/D-grade level (candidate A) — these have been selected to illustrate particular strengths and limitations
- example candidate responses at the A-grade level (candidate B) — such answers demonstrate thorough knowledge, a good understanding and an ability to deal with the issues raised by the questions

Examiner's comments

All candidate responses are followed by examiner's comments. These are preceded by the icon *e*. They indicate where credit is due and, in the weaker answer, they also point out areas for improvement, specific problems and common errors such as poor time management, lack of clarity, weak or non-existent development, irrelevance, misinterpretation of the question and mistaken meanings of terms. The comments also indicate how each example answer would be marked in an actual exam.

Assessment objectives

Examination boards use the term 'assessment objective' (AO) to refer to the different types of skills that you might be expected to demonstrate in examinations. Your teacher might have told you about AO1, AO2 and AO3 skills:
- AO1 refers to knowledge and understanding.
- AO2 refers to analysis and evaluation and the application of knowledge to novel situations.
- AO3 refers to knowledge and understanding of research methods and practical psychology.

You should not worry too much about these different skills in the examination. In most cases the wording of the question will lead you to demonstrate the necessary skills. Only the following two types of question require you to think about AO skills:
- 'Describe and evaluate', 'discuss' or 'compare' for 12 marks: whatever the wording of the 12-mark question, 4 marks are for description (AO1) and 8 marks are for evaluation, analysis and application (AO2). In a 12-mark question, you should aim to present a balance of description and evaluation/analysis/application.
- 'Briefly discuss' for 3, 4 or 5 marks: here, there would normally be 1 or 2 marks for description (AO1) and 2 or 3 marks for evaluation, analysis and application (AO2).

Child development

Social development

(a) In a study of children's friendship, a researcher compared stories written by 5-year-old girls and 5-year-old boys about their 'best friend'. Working alone, she categorised each story as either 'intimacy-focused' or 'activity-focused'.

    (i) Use your knowledge of research into children's friendships to propose a suitable research hypothesis for this study.   (2 marks)

    (ii) Identify *one* methodological limitation of this study.   (1 mark)

(b) (i) Describe *one* effect of institutionalisation.   (3 marks)

    (ii) Briefly discuss the effect you have identified in your answer to part (i).   (2 marks)

(c) Discuss Bowlby's work on attachment.   (12 marks)

Total: 20 marks

(a) For a 2-mark hypothesis in part (i), you need a testable statement in which the variables are clearly specified. Part (ii) requires only the briefest answer. In cases like this, where the description of the study includes a limitation, you would not get marks for proposing another possible, but unknown, limitation. For example, if you said that the type of sample was a limitation, you would not get any credit because we are not told anything about the sample.

(b) In part (i) you should describe one relevant effect in some detail. Be careful not to fall into the trap of giving several different effects — this would be a waste of time. In part (ii), you need to offer some evaluation or analysis. A couple of brief points or one issue in a bit more detail will suffice.

(c) You need to show fairly concise knowledge of Bowlby's work as there are only 4 marks for description/knowledge. The other 8 marks are for evaluation/analysis, i.e. presenting strengths and limitations and using evidence to support what you say. In this context 'work' could refer to theory and also to research.

■ ■ ■

Answer to question 1: candidate A

(a) (i) There is an association between the sex of the child and the story they write.

    ✏ Here the candidate correctly predicts an association between the variables, gaining 1 mark. The independent variable is sufficiently specified by the word 'sex' as this could only mean whether the children are male or female, but the dependent variable is not clearly defined. Had the candidate explained the two possible outcomes for the story (activity-based or intimacy-based), this would have been

question

worth the full 2 marks. Note that a hypothesis worded in terms of *differences* between numbers of males and females would also be credit-worthy.

(ii) One limitation with the study is the boys and girls might have different views about friends, even if they are the same age.

📝 The candidate has not realised the basic flaw in the study. This answer is hinting (not very well) at a possible confounding variable and, in any case, is confused. No mark is awarded here.

(b) (i) One likely effect is developmental delay, meaning a child has lower cognitive ability than non-institutionalised children of the same age. Reading and language ability would all be slowed if the child lives in an institution and there may be evidence of poorly developed social skills etc.

📝 This answer gives one effect and expands on it sufficiently for the full 3 marks.

(ii) The delay effect depends on what facilities and toys there are and not just on where they are etc.

📝 The critical comment is briefly explained but not fully explored. It certainly looks as if the candidate knows the answer, i.e. the effect is more likely to be due to the impoverished environment in some institutions than on the institutionalisation itself. Often, candidates assume examiners will 'fill in the rest' but it really is up to the candidate to make the point. Only 1 mark is awarded for this part.

(c) Bowlby was famous for saying that mother love is as important as vitamins and that children who did not have mother love would grow up to be damaged and violent. He interviewed teenagers in a juvenile detention centre who had been separated from mothers and noted how they were more likely to be delinquent as teenagers. However, we do not know if they really remembered being separated. Bowlby filmed children whose mothers went into hospital and found that they often could not get back with their mother. They would not look at her and found it difficult to trust people.

At the time Bowlby was speaking about his theory, not many people went to nursery. These days they do and they are not all damaged psychologically, so it is unlikely that his theory is relevant nowadays. Also, many people who are not separated from mothers do not grow up to be thieves and so there must be other reasons. In praise of Bowlby, it was good that he drew attention to childhood experience as important for future health and behaviour.

📝 This is quite a brief answer. The basic idea of long-term consequences is worth 1 mark and there is probably just enough description of the 44 thieves study for another mark. The point that follows is meant to be a criticism of the study, but it is insufficiently explained. Here there should be a full explanation of how the data was retrospective and therefore unreliable. The candidate gets a little confused about the Robertson studies; Bowlby used this evidence but did not carry out the research. However, the basic point that this is further evidence in general support of Bowlby's views is worthy of 1 mark. The final paragraph is also creditworthy. Although a little anecdotal (phrased in everyday terms) and poorly argued, these are reasonable points and, taken as a whole, worth another 2 marks. This answer is fairly typical of the average-to-poor band (AO1 = 2, AO2 = 3).

Total for this question: 10 out of 20 marks

■ ■ ■

Answer to question 1: candidate B

(a) (i) There will be a difference in the numbers of boys and girls writing activity-based stories and intimacy-based stories.

🖉 Here the hypothesis is testable and includes reference to both variables, so the candidate gets the full 2 marks. It would have been nice to see a directional hypothesis as research into friendship would allow for a prediction that boys' friendship is more about shared activity and girls' friendship is more about intimacy. However, the hypothesis here is technically correct and testable.

(ii) One problem is lack of reliability. The researcher is the only person categorising, so she might be subjective.

🖉 This is a good answer that is straight to the point and worth 1 mark.

(b) (i) One effect might be developmental delay, which means retarded development. Institutionalised children often have cognitive problems, e.g. poor reading etc.

🖉 An appropriate effect is given but the description/elaboration is limited. This answer is awarded 2 marks.

(ii) Evidence for this effect was demonstrated by the ERA group research with Romanian orphans. Rutter thought that adoption could overcome the negative effects. However, this seems to be possible only if a child is adopted before 6 months of age.

🖉 The discussion is brief but well done. Evidence (the ERA research) is used effectively here, first to support the effect given and then in reference to Rutter's original position and the counter-argument. This answer gains the full 2 marks.

(c) Bowlby was known for his theory of maternal deprivation. He stated that children should have a warm and uninterrupted bond with a single person, usually mother, for the first 2 years or else they would be delinquent and have other negative effects. Bowlby believed that children have an innate desire to stay close to this one figure, which helps them survive. He was a psychoanalyst and his evidence came from studying monkeys and 44 juvenile delinquents. These were boys Bowlby studied retrospectively using interviews with them and their parents. He found that many of them recalled they had been maternally separated and

17 eventually showed affectionless behaviour. He thought that if the attachment was broken or delayed in the critical 2 years, the damage would last for ever.

Critics of Bowlby say he confused deprivation with privation, which was actually what happened to the monkeys who had no mother at all when they were infants. Privation is never having had a bond, whereas deprivation is when you have a bond and then it is broken. According to Rutter, privation is much more severe than deprivation. At least if a child has had chance to form a bond at some time, he or she has some idea of loving relationships and does not grow up to be an affectionless psychopath.

Another problem for Bowlby is that other researchers showed how children do not have one single attachment and it does not have to be the mother. For example, Schaffer and Emerson in Glasgow found most children have multiple attachment figures, often including the father, and Freud and Dann found that seriously traumatised, separated children can form substitute attachments. It has also been shown that even late adopted children can form satisfactory and loving attachments, as in the case of the deprived Koluchova twins whose adult relationships were normal and happy. Bowlby's study of juvenile thieves was also retrospective and therefore not sound evidence — it is likely that the boys' recall of childhood events was not reliable.

The first paragraph is a concise yet detailed account of the main points of Bowlby's work. Although the terms 'monotropy' and 'critical period' are not used explicitly, these ideas are clearly described. There is reference to the negative effects of deprivation, innate desire for proximity and the 44 thieves study. Although Harlow's research is mistakenly attributed to Bowlby, the content of the first paragraph nevertheless scores the full 4 marks for AO1. In the next paragraph, the candidate thoroughly explores the point about confusion between deprivation and privation; the terms are clarified and the difference in consequences for future relationships is explained. In the final paragraph, the candidate argues against the focus on the mother, monotropy and the critical period, using counter-evidence effectively. The final brief point about the 44 thieves study is just sufficiently elaborated for a further mark. Note that had this candidate not already gained the maximum AO1 marks for knowledge, he or she could have been awarded 1 mark for description of evidence here. The discussion is awarded 7 out of 8 AO2 marks and the answer as a whole fits the top-band descriptor (AO1 = 4, AO2 = 7).

Total for this question: 18 out of 20 marks

Child development
Cognitive development

(a) Two groups of children were asked to solve a puzzle by fitting 30 shapes together. One group of children performed the task alongside an adult, who made helpful suggestions at the start and then gradually withdrew support. Another group of children performed the task alone. One week later, all the children were tested on their ability to solve a similar puzzle alone.

    (i)   What influence on cognitive development is being investigated in this study?   (1 mark)

    (ii) Identify the independent variable in this study.   (1 mark)

    (iii) Suggest *one* measure that could be used as the dependent variable.   (1 mark)

    (iv) Identify the experimental design in this study.   (1 mark)

(b) Outline and briefly discuss the information processing approach to cognitive development.   (4 marks)

(c) Describe and evaluate Piaget's theory of cognitive development.   (12 marks)

Total: 20 marks

(a) All parts require only the briefest answer. You do not even need to write in full sentences if you know the correct term/name.

(b) You have to provide an outline, which is just a brief description, and then offer some discussion point (evaluation or comment). This could be one briefly elaborated point or a brief mention of two points.

(c) This looks like a dream question because every candidate knows a lot about Piaget's theory. However, you need to remember that there are only 4 marks for knowledge and description of the theory; the remaining 8 marks are for evaluation. A common error in a 12-mark Piaget question is to spend too long on description and run out of time for discussion or evaluation. Note that the question is asking you to describe and evaluate the theory and not the evidence. In a 12-mark question, you can usually gain one AO1 mark for describing a relevant study, but do not describe lots of studies in detail, unless of course the question is asking you to describe and evaluate evidence.

■ ■ ■

Answer to question 2: candidate A

(a) (i) Problem-solving is being studied.

    The candidate has not understood the key difference between the two conditions and therefore gains no marks.

(ii) The independent variable is the support that is given or not given.

2 The independent variable is correct despite the mistake in part (i), so **1** mark is awarded.

(iii) They could record how long it takes put the shapes together.

2 This is a good idea, which gains **1** mark.

(iv) Independent measures — different in each condition and not matched.

2 It would be enough to simply name the design here. The candidate gets **1** mark.

(b) The information processing approach suggests that cognitive development is about the amount of ability increasing with age, e.g. memory gets more efficient with age. Bee says that with age children use better strategies because they have better metamemory.

2 This answer is awarded **2** marks for the outline but there is no discussion. This is a fairly common mistake in 'Briefly discuss...' questions.

(c) Piaget's theory was a stage theory. There are four stages, from birth until 12 years when schema have fully developed. At each stage thinking was different. In the sensori-motor stage, children are egocentric and do not have object permanence. If a toy is covered they will not carry on and look for it. In the pre-operational stage, children are still egocentric but now have object permanence. They cannot do the three mountain task because they cannot see another's point of view. They cannot conserve either. In the next stage, they can conserve so can tell that a long, thin glass holds the same as a short, fat glass. They can do class inclusion tasks, but at this time they can only reason about real things and cannot do abstract reasoning and hypothesising about 'what would happen if...' This arises in the formal operations stage when the child can do abstract thought.

Piaget has been criticised for his methods because he did most experiments himself with his own children. He did not have proper controls or use statistics. Others have copied his work and found different results. For example, Bower turned out the lights; Hughes did a different egocentrism experiment and the results were different. Children aged 3 or 4 could put the doll where the policeman could not see him, showing they did not have egocentrism.

2 The candidate has realised the problem here and tried to trim the content down to a manageable size. The first paragraph is a description of Piaget's stage theory. Each stage is noted and the candidate correctly shows the basic characteristics of thinking at each stage. Although it is not well written, there are no errors and most key concepts (e.g. egocentrism and object permanence) are briefly explained. It is a shame that there is not more on general aspects of Piaget's theory, such as adaptation and schema development, but this would have been a lot to expect in such limited time. The full **4** marks are awarded for AO1. In the second paragraph, several evaluation points are presented although most are not fully developed. The methodological criticisms could have been expanded with an explanation of why these issues are a problem and how they might have affected Piaget's conclusions. The alternative research and findings could have been compared to Piaget's work in much more detail by noting the key differences between the methods. For example, why was Hughes able to demonstrate that 3 or 4-year-old children were not egocentric when Piaget did not? In all, this paragraph is awarded 1 mark for the methodological points and 1 mark for the alternatives. Overall, the answer appears to be at the top of the average-to-poor band (AO1 = 4, AO2 = 2).

Total for this question: 11 out of 20 marks

■ ■ ■

Answer to question 2: candidate B

(a) (i) The researcher is studying scaffolding.

e This answer gains 1 mark.

(ii) The independent variable is whether the child has the support of scaffolding or not.

e The independent variable is correct and the candidate specifies both conditions, gaining 1 mark.

(iii) The number of shapes fitted together in 1 minute.

e This is a plausible idea even though we do not really know whether 1 minute would be an appropriate time or not. The candidate gets 1 mark.

(iv) Independent design.

e 1 mark is awarded.

(b) Information processing theorists see children's thinking as similar to computer processing. This is a problem in child development because children develop in a social context and are active in their problem-solving. Children might also solve problems in novel or unusual ways, which a computer could never do.

e 1 description mark (AO1) is awarded for a sensible point about information processing theory. Unfortunately, this has not been expanded by further description. The discussion is brief but relevant and well applied to children's thinking, so worth 2 AO2 marks. In all, this answer scores 3 marks.

(c) Piaget was an influential theorist whose ideas, such as discovery learning, have been much used by classroom teachers. His stage theory explored the development of thinking and described how child's schemas develop from being simple, motor schemas into an abstract understanding. He believed that due to active experience, knowledge adapts through assimilation and accommodation. In the sensori-motor stage, a baby has no object permanence, meaning he or she cannot understand that an object continues to exist when it is out of sight. In the pre-operational stage, there are many constraints. The child is egocentric and thinking is ruled by outward appearance so the child cannot conserve volume, mass etc. In the concrete operational stage, these abilities are developed, the child can imagine another's point of view and can use logic with concrete problems. In the final stage, there is abstract, hypothetical reasoning.

Piaget's ideas about active experience and readiness to learn have been criticised by people who argue that sociocultural influences such as friends, family, peers and teachers affect cognitive development and that it can be accelerated. Vygotsky did not agree with Piaget that the child was like a scientist or sole explorer. Instead, he saw the child as an apprentice to the skills and knowledge of his or her culture. Other researchers claimed that Piaget underestimated children's abilities because he always assumed that failure to perform a task meant that the child was unable to perform it. Critics thought Piaget's theory was based on misinterpretation of the results of his studies. For example, in conservation experiments Piaget asked a child the same question twice, perhaps leading them to assume the first answer was wrong, so explaining the second incorrect answer. In short, Piaget himself was egocentric, failing to see his experiments from the point of view of the child.

Although Piaget's ideas are much used in education, they can lead to problems. If teachers always waited for a child to be ready to learn, some children would never progress. Also, children left to discover things on their own may not have enough structure to their lessons and may waste a lot of time. However, Piaget is to be acclaimed as a key figure in child development.

This is an excellent top-band answer with a good balance of description and evaluation. The candidate starts well by making a simple evaluative comment about educational application of the theory. This gains AO2 marks. The rest of the first paragraph is a concise and yet full account of the main aspects of the theory, including key concepts and detail of the stages. Note there is no description of evidence. As there is ample descriptive material without detail of studies, it would have been a waste of time in this case. The candidate gains 4 AO1 marks for knowledge of the theory. In the second paragraph, he/she makes two creditworthy points in the first sentence. The comparison with Vygotsky, although not specifically required in the question, is a useful way to gain more analysis/evaluation marks. The points about underestimation, misinterpretation and Piaget's own egocentrism are relevant and well expressed and the example of conservation is used to maximum effect. The final paragraph is interesting and unusual as candidates usually tend to assume Piaget's ideas always had a positive effect on education. This candidate usefully presents some potential negative implications of the theory, returning to his or her first point about education. In all, this is a knowledgeable and well-argued answer with a good balance and some insightful evaluation. The maximum 8 AO2 marks are awarded for evaluation, analysis, comparison and discussion of implications (AO1 = 4, AO2 = 8).

Total for this question: 19 out of 20 marks

Child development
Moral development

(a) Children hear a story about Ed who has the chance to help his classmate tidy up the classroom. If Ed stays behind to do the tidying, he will miss having chocolate biscuits at playtime. Children are asked individually whether Ed should help and, if so, why. Use your knowledge of Eisenberg's theory of moral reasoning to:

    (i)   Identify the type of moral dilemma facing Ed.   (1 mark)

    (ii) Give *one* likely response of a child in the hedonistic stage.
           Explain your answer.   (2 marks)

    (iii) Give *one* likely response of a child in the approval stage.
           Explain your answer.   (2 marks)

(b) Briefly evaluate the moral comparison technique.   (3 marks)

(c) Discuss Gilligan's work on moral development.   (12 marks)

Total: 20 marks

(a) Part (i) requires the briefest answer. You do not even need to write a sentence if you know the correct term. In parts (ii) and (iii), you have to suggest a possible response and explain how that response demonstrates hedonistic or approval-oriented reasoning.

(b) This is a methodology question where you need to evaluate a method of studying moral development. Here you can take a depth or breadth approach: you could choose one issue and expand on it in some detail or you could consider more than one issue in less depth. Whichever approach you take, be careful not to spend to long on this question as it is only worth 3 marks.

(c) This is a straightforward question where you are looking for 4 AO1 marks and 8 AO2 marks. This means you should aim to spend more time on discussion than on description. The question asks about 'Gilligan's work', which means it will be legitimate to discuss both theory and research in the answer. Although there is no explicit requirement for you to make comparisons with alternative views (for example, Kohlberg), this is often a good way to get evaluation marks.

■ ■ ■

Answer to question 3: candidate A

(a) (i) Ed has to decide whether he should hurt the other child's feelings. This is his dilemma so morally he might be worried that he will get punished for not helping the boy.

The candidate has attempted an answer but has not recognised that this is a *prosocial dilemma*, so no mark is given.

(ii) A child in the hedonistic stage might say 'Ed should not help' because he would miss the biscuits, which is all he thinks about, what he wants.

 The likely response is appropriate and there is just about enough explanation for the full 2 marks. It would have been better if the candidate had explained fully what hedonistic meant, but it is implied here.

(iii) A child in the approval stage would say 'Ed should help' because it would be nice of him.

 Again, this is an appropriate response. However, in this case, the explanation is not really adequate because there is no direct reference to the most important aspect of the approval stage, i.e. that other people would think well of him. Only 1 mark out of 2 is awarded.

(b) In the moral comparison technique, Piaget asked children to listen to two stories and then to choose who was the naughtiest person in the stories. In one story a little boy called John knocked over one cup on purpose and in another Henry smashed 15 cups by mistake. Most children under the age of 7 chose Henry because he had caused the most damage. Older children tended to chose John because he did it on purpose. This shows that under the age of 7 most children are moral realists and judge by consequence, as opposed to older children who judge by intention (moral relativism). Alternatively, the younger children maybe could not remember the stories well.

 Although this candidate clearly knows a lot about the technique, the content is almost entirely descriptive; there is a single brief evaluation point at the end, almost like an afterthought. This answer is awarded 1 mark out of 3, although the candidate probably thought he or she had answered it well.

(c) Gilligan studied women having abortions at a clinic, which was a good thing to do because it was a real-life dilemma, not hypothetical, and therefore had high ecological validity. She found they showed stages of reasoning. Some women focused only on what they wanted: this was called the self-interest stage. Others thought that the needs of other people were most important, like the baby or the father. This is called the sacrificing stage. This led Gilligan, who was a woman, to propose the ethic of care which is a description of female moral reasoning. She was a student of Kohlberg and thought he was biased in favour of males and there-fore she said that women and men reasoned differently (care or justice) but that one was not any better than the other, unlike Kohlberg who thought men reasoned at a higher level.

Gilligan's view was good because until her work came along the study of moral development had been just looking at male morality, e.g. Kohlberg's research. However, some have argued that she too was biased because she only studied women. If she had asked men about abortion, she might have found that they reasoned a bit like women when it comes to such a sensitive issue. Walker said this was the case.

✐ The first point about ecological validity is a sensible one and gets AO2 credit. The description that follows shows some knowledge of Gilligan's work. There is confusion over the three levels (not two stages) and the names given here are not exactly correct. The answer gains 3 rather generous AO1 marks for content that is slightly inaccurate and lacking in detail. At the end of the first paragraph, an AO2 mark is awarded for the comparison with Kohlberg. In the second paragraph, there is further comparison with Kohlberg and a valid point about the relevance of the type of the dilemma. Indeed, this is what Walker found, although the candidate does not offer any further information about Walker's study, which could have gained more marks, either AO1 for description or AO2 for analysis of what the results showed in relation to Gilligan's work. This is a respectable average-to-good band response (AO1 = 3, AO2 = 3).

Total for this question: 10 out of 20 marks

■ ■ ■

Answer to question 3: candidate B

(a) (i) This is a prosocial dilemma.

✐ 1 mark is awarded.

(ii) A hedonistic child would say Ed should not help. Instead, he should be hedonistic and do what is most pleasurable for him, i.e. have the chocolate biscuits.

✐ A clear and well-explained answer that is worth the full 2 marks.

(iii) An approval stage child would say Ed should help because then the teacher would think he was a good person and praise him.

✐ This is another sound answer that deserves the full 2 marks.

(b) The original moral comparison technique (John and Henry and the cups) was used by Piaget. It requires reasoning about who is more naughty in a hypothetical situation. The big problem with how Piaget did the experiment was that he varied the amount of damage and whether the damage was on purpose or not at the same time. This means he had two independent variables and did not really know which one influenced the children's decisions. This was a basic flaw in his design. Nelson did a variation where she used four stories, which improved the technique.

✐ This is a direct answer. The candidate chooses an issue and explains it thoroughly enough for the full 3 marks.

(c) Gilligan did not agree with Kolhberg that female reasoning was less sophisticated than male reasoning. She suggested that women had an ethic of care which led

them to focus on care for others and empathy. In contrast, men had an ethic of justice which led them to focus on justice and the law. She argued that this is the reason females were often at Kohlberg's level three and males at level four. In short, she argued Kohlberg's system was male-biased.

In her own research, Gilligan studied 29 women considering abortions using structured interviews. This method means everyone gets the same questions and therefore there is less researcher bias. As this was a real-life dilemma, this research has high ecological validity which is an improvement on the hypothetical dilemmas used by other researchers. Through her interviews, Gilligan found three types of reasoning. The least sophisticated was self-interest where women only thought about themselves ('It will ruin my life.') This is similar to Kohlberg's reward stage reasoning or Eisenberg's hedonistic reasoning. In the self-sacrifice stage, women think only about others like the unborn baby, their partner etc. In the most sophisticated stage, non-violence, they try to consider all points of view and the main concern is with not hurting anyone.

This research has been criticised though. Perhaps Gilligan should have studied men's view on abortion too. Indeed, Walker found that the type of reasoning depended on the type of dilemma. Walker's research showed that both men and women can use justice-based and care-based reasoning in different situations. This means Gilligan's views on ethic of care and ethic of justice were perhaps over-simplified.

There are some similarities between Gilligan and Freudian theory in that they both argue there are differences between male and female morality. However, Gilligan would not agree that females are morally inferior, as Freud stated.

This is a well-constructed answer that starts with a comparison with Kohlberg which gains AO2 credit. In the first and second paragraphs there is sufficient knowledge for 4 AO1 marks. The concepts of ethic of care and ethic of justice are clearly outlined, the stages are correctly named and outlined and there is some description of the abortion clinic study. The evaluative points about real-life versus hypothetical dilemmas and the structured interview are embedded in the description of the Gilligan study. Although there is no requirement to integrate evaluation and description, it is does make the answer flow better and appear more sophisticated overall. Note how the candidate gains more AO2 credit by quickly comparing Gilligan's levels with those of Kohlberg and Eisenberg. In the third paragraph, the candidate explores Walker's criticism of Gilligan's conclusions, gaining more AO2 credit. In the last paragraph, there is a neat comparison with psychodynamic theory, giving both a similarity and a difference. Although not a long answer, there is substantial evaluation, analysis and comparison for the top band (AO1 = 4, AO2 = 8).

Total for this question: 20 out of 20 marks

Applied options
Cognition and law

(a) Using your knowledge of psychology, outline and briefly discuss *one* way in which children's ability to recall events differs from that of adults. **(4 marks)**

(b) Identify and briefly explain *two* implications of the false memory debate. **(4 marks)**

(c) Discuss one way of improving eyewitness recall. Refer to evidence in your answer. **(12 marks)**

Total: 20 marks

(a) There are 2 marks for an outline and 2 marks for a brief discussion or evaluative comment. Note that only one difference in recalling events is required, so if you gave more than one you would be credited for the best. However, this would be a waste of time, so it is not an advisable strategy. The question refers to 'knowledge of psychology' so the answer should have some basis in research or theory and not be purely common sense.

(b) Here you must give two implications. Often, candidates answer questions like this rather vaguely, letting the two points get muddled together. Then there is a danger that the examiner will only spot one of them. To be sure, you should separate the two implications clearly. Start with 'The first implication is…' and then, on a new line, 'The second implication is…'.

(c) Your answer must focus on one way of improving recall. It is legitimate to refer to other possible ways as part of the discussion, as long as you do not lose sight of the focus of the discussion. Note the specific requirement for evidence here. If you do not refer to any studies, your mark would be limited to a maximum of 8. The references to studies need not be detailed descriptions; the findings would be sufficient. Although not essential, it helps if you can add weight to your presentation of evidence by using the researcher's name. It makes the whole answer more credible and less anecdotal.

■ ■ ■

Answer to question 4: candidate A

(a) Children make up things more than adults because they have such good imaginations. This means that their recall of events is sometimes unreliable. It is also found that children's memories are more distorted through talking about it afterwards.

> The first sentence is anecdotal, but fortunately there is a reference to lack of reliability in the second sentence. This basic point gains 1 mark. In the next sentence there is a brief point about the influence of post-event discussion, which could easily have been expanded. As it is, this gains a further mark, so a total of 2 marks are awarded here.

4

question

(b) One implication is that at least judges and professionals are aware that some of the recovered memories may not actually have happened. We should not always assume it is a true account of the child's past. Another implication is that families can be destroyed. There would be no going back from that.

> The first implication is valid and coherently explained, so worth 2 marks. The second point is much briefer and there is no clear link to the debate. This point is not sufficiently explained for credit.

(c) One way to improve eyewitness recall is by restoring the context. People tend to remember more when they are in the same context as when they learned the information in the first place. This was done by Baddeley in the underwater study, where people who learned either on land or underwater and then had to recall either on land or underwater were found to recall more of the nonsense words if they were in the same place where they first learned them. However, this study is not ecologically valid because it is unlikely a person would witness something and then be in the same place when they recall it. They would probably be in a police station. Also, eyewitnesses have much more important information to recall than nonsense words, so there is more pressure on them to recall than there was on the divers in the underwater study. Restoring the context could be done by asking the witness to imagine what they felt like at the time. This is done in the cognitive interview and results show it leads to much better recall compared with normal interviews or hypnosis (Geiselman).

Another way to improve recall would be to make sure the witness does not talk to anyone after the event because then there would be less chance of post-event contamination. Of course this would mean keeping the person in isolation which is not really possible, so in practice this is not going to be a helpful way of improving recall. Another way is to use modern composite systems for constructing faces rather than the old-fashioned identikit system. Modern systems such as VIPER do not have crude lines between features and can be adjusted slightly to get the best likeness. Therefore, there are several ways to improve recall.

> This answer starts well and gets AO1 credit for outlining restoring context as an appropriate way of improving recall. The evidence is probably a study that was covered in the AS year but that does not matter. It is relevant here and is properly described, so worthy of AO1 credit. There is an evaluative comment about ecological validity. Candidates often use this term but do not get credit because they fail to explain what they mean in relation to the study presented. This candidate gives well-elaborated explanations and gains 2 AO2 marks. There follows a valid point about how context can be restored in the cognitive interview, which gains AO1 credit and, finally, a brief reference to findings in relation to effectiveness for AO2. In the following paragraph, the candidate gives two additional ways of improving recall. Unfortunately, these receive no credit because the question specifies just one way. In this case, the examiner has credited whichever material

benefits the candidate more. Unfortunately, it means that precious time has been wasted, which might have been better spent elsewhere (AO1 = 3, AO2 = 3).

Total for this question: 10 out of 20 marks

■ ■ ■

Answer to question 4: candidate B

(a) One difference is that adults get less confused about where their memory comes from. This is known as source monitoring. Adults tend to remember better whether something really happened to them or whether they heard about it. This is shown in the Mr Science study where children thought they had seen science demonstrations they had only heard about. However, in real life children have to remember much more important things (e.g. abuse) than in studies.

🖉 This is a comprehensive answer. Source monitoring is named and fully explained, with the difference between adult and child recall made absolutely clear. For discussion, the candidate has used evidence to back up the point and then offered a critical comment about the evidence. This answer deserves the full 4 marks.

(b) One implication is that Loftus's theory of reconstructive memory may not be right. Another implication of the debate is ethical. If memories are often false, as Loftus argues, then some cases of 'recovered memory' where people accuse parents of childhood abuse may not really be recovered memories at all. In which case, parents might be convicted when they did not do anything.

🖉 This candidate separates the two implications and offers one theoretical and one ethical. The theoretical implication is not really explained at all, but the ethical point is more detailed. The first point is awarded 1 mark and the second, 2 marks.

(c) One way of improving eyewitness recall is to use the cognitive interview. This is a special technique devised in the 1980s and now used by specially trained police officers. It involves four strategies. The first is reinstating the context. Context has been shown to aid recall, for example, Malpass and Devine asked participants to recall an act of vandalism and found that those who were told about the time and date showed better recall than a control group. To restore a witness's context, they could be told the date and asked to remember how they felt that day and what had happened earlier. Another strategy involves recalling in a different order, going back in time rather than chronologically. So the witness would be asked, 'What happened before that?' instead of 'Then what happened?' Another strategy is asking about events from another perspective, for example asking what a person on the other side of the room might have seen. Finally the witness should give the smallest details, even when they might seem unimportant. Tiny details might overlap with other details and lead to more important information. Of course, not all police officers would have the necessary training to interview in this way, so the cognitive interview cannot always be used.

4

question

In a study by Geiselman (1986) it was found that the cognitive interview technique led to more correct details being recalled, suggesting it is a highly effective technique. However, others have disagreed that all four components of the cognitive interview are necessary. For example, Milne found that the most helpful aspects were context and recalling all details, with the others less important.

It also might work better in some situations than others. For obvious reasons, it is better for helping people recall events, where there is a sequence of things happening, than for aiding recall of faces. Face recognition seems to depend on many factors (top-down and bottom-up) and is a more complex process, so the cognitive interview is less helpful there. Also, according to Freudian theory, witnesses to horrific events like car crashes might repress the detail into the unconscious. This would mean that the cognitive interview would not help access the memories so perhaps would be less useful in such cases. Horrific details that have been repressed might be more easily accessed through psychoanalysis.

✍ This is a high-level response which is clearly presented. There is detailed description of all aspects of the technique and reference to two studies. In this case, the description of the technique itself is worth the maximum AO1 marks, although had it been presented in less detail, credit could have been awarded for knowledge of evidence. In the first paragraph there are two creditworthy evaluative points: use of evidence (Malpass and Devine) to support the point about the importance of context and brief comment about not all officers being trained. Although this is not verified here, it is nevertheless a plausible point. In the second paragraph, there is further use of evidence and the point about the necessity to use all four aspects of the technique. Both these points are worthy of AO2 credit. In the final paragraph, two highly relevant points about face recognition and repression are discussed effectively, showing an impressively integrated understanding of the whole topic area. This paragraph is awarded 4 AO2 marks. Altogether, this response fits the description for a top-band answer (AO1 = 4, AO2 = 8).

Total for this question: 19 out of 20 marks

Applied options

Schizophrenia and mood disorders

(a) (i) Outline what is meant by *bipolar depression*.   (2 marks)

   (ii) Briefly explain *one* problem that might arise when using cognitive
         therapy in cases of bipolar depression.   (2 marks)

(b) Pat has been diagnosed as having schizophrenia.

   (i)   Give two symptoms that Pat might be experiencing.   (2 marks)

   (ii) With reference to labelling, explain the possible effect of
         diagnosis on Pat.   (2 marks)

   (iii) Compare biological and cognitive explanations for Pat's
         schizophrenia.   (12 marks)

Total: 20 marks

The most important thing to remember in this question is to look carefully at each
sub-section before you start. Candidates often get mixed up and write about schizophrenia when the question sub-section is about mood disorders or vice versa.

(a) Part (i) requires a brief answer. The greatest risk here is confusion between bipolar
and unipolar disorder. There are at least two valid answers to part (ii), which should
be fairly obvious to those candidates who know that bipolar disorder involves
bouts of mania and cognitive therapy involves reasoning and discussion. Candidates
who are confused about either may struggle here.

(b) In part (i), only the briefest answer is required. There is no need even to write in
sentences and there are lots of symptoms to choose from. Part (ii) requires an
understanding of the term *labelling* and the consequences of it. Again, only a brief
answer is required. In part (iii), it is important to aim for a mix of similarities and
differences so there is plenty to discuss. As usual in 12-mark questions, there is a
maximum of 4 marks for knowledge, in this case of the two explanations, with the
remaining marks for comparison and use of evidence. As always, it is possible to get
at least 1 mark for knowledge of relevant evidence, although in this case it is
unlikely that candidates will need to scratch around for extra AO1 marks. A
common mistake in 'compare' questions is to stray from comparison and spend too
much time evaluating each theory or explanation separately. Answers that do not
focus clearly on comparison cannot score in the top mark band. Answers with no
direct comparison tend to be limited to the bottom two bands.

■ ■ ■

question 5

The first paragraph includes a reasonable outline of the biological explanation, which is worth 2 marks. Unfortunately, the reference to twin studies and how they provide evidence for the biological explanation is incomplete and so does not gain AO2 credit. The outline of the cognitive explanation appears to relate more to mood disorders than schizophrenia, although 1 mark is awarded for reference to 'distorted thinking'. The second paragraph is awarded 1 AO2 mark for use of evidence, some of which is rather vague, to support the biological explanation. The comparison point about how much evidence there is for each explanation is weak but just about worthy of another AO2 mark. The final short paragraph contains a valid point and is awarded AO2 credit. Overall, this is not a strong answer; there is confusion and lack of detailed explanation. The candidate does, however, try to focus on comparison, some of which is effective. This is an average-to-poor answer (AO1 = 3, AO2 = 3).

Total for this question: 10 out of 20 marks

■ ■ ■

Answer to question 5: candidate B

(a) (i) Bipolar depression is where the mood disorder is at both ends of the mood spectrum, with both depression and mania alternating.

This is a good answer, worthy of the full 2 marks. The idea of alternation between mania and depression is explicit.

(ii) Bipolar patients become completely irrational and unreasonable in the mania phase. At this time they cannot have a sensible conversation, which would be necessary for cognitive therapy where the client and therapist have to work together to find solutions.

A good reason is given here and it is fully explained. This is a 2-mark answer.

(b) (i) Two symptoms are hallucinations and delusions.

The full 2 marks are awarded.

(ii) Labelling is where a person who has been diagnosed with a disorder starts to behave in the way expected of someone with that label. Once Pat knows she has schizophrenia, she may start to behave in an even more disturbed way and the label will come true — a self-fulfilling prophecy. This happened in Rosenhan's study when people were labelled with schizophrenia and people expected them to be odd and perceived odd behaviour even when they were doing normal things.

This answer is easily worth the full 2 marks. Indeed, the first two sentences would have been quite sufficient.

(iii) Biological psychologists explain schizophrenia in terms of inherited schizophrenic genes and unbalances in neurotransmitters. Dopamine levels appear to be excessive in people who have schizophrenia. Evidence to support the dopamine hypothesis comes from finding that blocking dopamine receptors with the medication chlorpromazine leads to a reduction of the symptoms of the disorder.

According to the cognitive explanation, distorted thinking leads to the development of the disorder. Cognitive researchers suggest that the problem may be due to the misperception of own thoughts as external stimuli, which would lead to hallucinatory symptoms. Evidence from a study by Stirling (1998) shows that patients with positive symptoms are less aware of their own output (for example, drawings they have produced) than non-sufferers, indicating a cognitive processing difficulty.

A key difference between the two explanations is their ability to explain the root cause of the disorder. The biological explanation offers a clear cause in the form of low dopamine and inheritance, while the cognitive explanation informs about the processing problems experienced by patients but does not in itself provide us with a cause. On closer inspection, however, we cannot be sure that high dopamine is indeed a cause; some have argued that raised levels may also be a symptom. If that is the case, perhaps neither explanation offers a clear cause.

Another difference lies in their implications for treatment. If we accept the biological explanation, this would logically lead to the use of some biological intervention as treatment. If, however, we assume that information processing is the main problem, this could point to the use of cognitive strategies to alter the patient's thinking. In practice, although biological treatments are relatively easy to apply in the form of medication, patients with schizophrenia are often difficult to treat with cognitive therapy because they sometimes have a poor grip on reality.

The main similarity between the two explanations is that they are both based on highly controlled scientific methods. Biopsychologists use laboratory research (such as chemical analysis) and cognitive psychologists also employ controlled manipulation of variables and rigorous data analysis. In this way, perhaps they could both be said to be reductionist, one focusing on discrete chemical function and the other on a specific cognitive ability. Perhaps in doing so, each loses sight of the whole experience of being a person with schizophrenia.

In summary, it is perhaps sensible to see these explanations as complementary rather than competing. The problem may have its root in chemical imbalance, which then leads to disordered cognitive processing.

e This is an exceptional top-band answer. The first two paragraphs offer a clear outline of each explanation, so the candidate gains the maximum 4 marks for description/knowledge. For each explanation there is also reference to supporting evidence, each of these references gaining AO2 credit. In the third paragraph, the candidate explores the issues of cause and effect, relating this well to the two explanations. Note how there is real discussion here, with the candidate taking one position at the start of the paragraph and working round to a counter-argument at the end. In all, this paragraph gains 3 AO2 marks. In the fourth paragraph, the candidate cleverly refers to implications for treatment, which makes the material on treatment relevant to explanation and thus keeps the content focused on the question. A common problem is for candidates to talk about treatment when they should be discussing explanations, without providing any link between the two. In all, this paragraph gains 2 AO2 marks, 1 for the different treatment strategies and 1 for the appropriateness of each for treating schizophrenia. The penultimate paragraph is worth a total of 4 AO2 marks; there are valid similarities in the form of methods and the broader issue of reductionism. Both these points are explained well and linked to each explanation. There is also an insightful comment about how each explanation tends to lose sight of the whole person. Although by now the candidate has accrued maximum marks, the final observation in the last paragraph is also worthy of AO2 credit. This is an outstandingly well-organised answer to a difficult question. There is a clear emphasis on comparison and the candidate has worked hard throughout to fully explain every point (AO1 = 4, AO2 = 8).

Total for this question: 20 out of 20 marks

Question Q6

Applied options
Stress and stress management

(a) Daniel copes with the stress of work by going out and having a laugh with his friends. Bernie copes with the stress of work by seeing his supervisor and organising a reduced workload.

  (i) **Distinguish between problem-focused and emotion-focused strategies. Refer to Daniel and Bernie in your answer.** (5 marks)

  (ii) **Bernie goes on a stress management course, where he takes part in biofeedback sessions. Outline biofeedback and suggest *one* limitation of the use of biofeedback for work-based stress such as Bernie's.** (3 marks)

(b) **Discuss the role of at least *two* personal variables in mediating responses to stress.** (12 marks)

Total: 20 marks

(a) Part (i) is asking you to do two things. First, you need to explain the difference between problem-focused and emotion-focused strategies. The easiest way to do this is to define each, then to explicitly point out a difference between them. You then need to refer to Daniel and Bernie by saying which type of strategy each of them is using. In part (ii), you need to provide a brief description of biofeedback and then briefly state one limitation. Note that this should not be a general limitation of biofeedback, but one that would apply particularly in Bernie's case, i.e. where stress is related to work.

(b) Here, there are 4 marks for knowledge and description of at least two personal variables, and 8 marks for discussion of their role in mediating responses to stress. The description marks should be obtained relatively easily as long as you choose relevant personal variables. The specification refers to personality types A, B and C, hardiness and locus of control. As usual in the 12-mark questions, it is possible to get at least 1 description mark for knowledge of a relevant study. The discussion should focus on the role of personal variables in mediating stress, for example how they make it easier or harder for a person to cope in stressful situations. You could refer to evidence to support what you say and to alternative factors that might affect responses to stress. You would also be able to gain marks by evaluating the evidence you present.

■ ■ ■

Answer to question 6: candidate A

(a) (i) Problem-focused gets to the heart of the problem, like Bernie is doing. Emotion-focused is more about not dealing with it. This is what Daniel is doing.

🖉 There is no clear definition of either type here, although an understanding of the difference is implicit. It is important to explain each point fully for maximum marks and, given that the answer is worth 5 marks, this candidate should have realised a more thorough answer was required. The answer gets 3 marks; both strategies are correctly linked to Daniel and Bernie and a difference between them is briefly noted.

(ii) Biofeedback is where people get feedback about their body as they are doing a task. This allows them to control their body. Bernie could then use this to deal with stress because when he feels his heart rate increasing he can cause it to be steady again and then not get upset.

🖉 There is some understanding of the technique here, although the candidate does not make it clear that it is autonomic function that is being monitored or that reinforcement is involved. The candidate seems to have missed the second part of the question, as there is no suggestion as to why it would be difficult for Bernie to use biofeedback for work-based stress. Only 1 mark out of 3 is awarded.

(b) Personal variables have a huge effect on dealing and coping with stress. Some people naturally have a personality that means that they can cope better with stress. These are type B personality as identified by Friedman and Rosenman. Type Bs are calm and laid back. They do not get upset easily and keep cool under pressure. On the other hand, type A people are the typical high-pressured executive types who get stressed easily. They seem to thrive on stress but eventually get burnt out by it and then begin to suffer from stress-related illness such as cancer and high blood pressure. In a study to support this, Friedman and Rosenman measured stress in middle-aged men and found that the personality type could be used to predict whether or not they would develop high blood pressure. In fact, men identified as type A by their colleagues were five times more likely to develop heart disorders than type Bs, so personality type affects response to stress.

Another personal variable that relates to this would be locus of control. This means how much you think you can control what happens to you. It is much better to believe that we have high control over what happens and then we do not get so stressed out. This was claimed by Rotter and he used a questionnaire, the locus of control scale.

🖉 This candidate correctly identifies types A and B and describes each type. The descriptions are a little anecdotal, but they are correct and therefore each is worthy of credit. An AO2 mark is awarded for explaining how personality type mediates the effects of stress, with type A being more likely to suffer stress-related illness. At the end of the paragraph, there is a brief description of the study, which can be awarded a further description mark. The findings of the study are used effectively for another AO2 mark. In the second paragraph, another relevant

variable – locus of control – is identified and outlined for 1 mark. It is a shame that the candidate does not use the terms *internal* and *external* and elaborate on how these two types of locus of control would mediate response to stress. No further marks are awarded as the candidate has not made it clear that a balance of internal and external is most healthy, and that an extreme at either end of the continuum can lead to stress. This is fairly typical of an answer at the top of the average-to-poor band (AO1 = 4, AO2 = 2).

Total for this question: 10 out of 20 marks

■ ■ ■

Answer to question 6: candidate B

(a) (i) Emotion-focused strategies tackle the response to the stress rather than the stress itself. Problem-focused strategies tackle the source of stress rather than the person's reaction to it. Daniel is using an emotion-focused strategy whereas Bernie's approach is to use a problem-focused way. Generally speaking, the problem-focused approach is more practical and more effective. It addresses the cause directly and doesn't simply involve putting off dealing with it till later.

✓ This is a full-mark answer. There is clear knowledge of the two strategies and the final sentence makes a clear distinction. Each type is correctly linked to Daniel's and Bernie's behaviour.

(ii) Biofeedback is a behavioural technique where patients are taught to monitor and control their own autonomic response (heart rate, muscle tension etc.) using reinforcement, for example when heart rate decreases back to normal. A machine is necessary for this and it is difficult to do when relaxation is needed without the necessary equipment. This is why is might not help Bernie when he is at work.

✓ This is a good answer. There is ample description in the first sentence and the candidate correctly identifies a problem — that the technique is hard to do without feedback and this would be impossible in a work situation. The full 3 marks are awarded.

(b) Not everyone responds to stress in the same way. One variable that mediates response to stress is hardiness, defined by Kobasa (1979) as a set of traits (commitment, control and challenge) that act as a buffer and enable a robust response to stress. Challenge allows a person to see potential stressors as opportunities rather than threats. This means that they see the positives to stress rather than just the negatives, so stress does not affect the person badly. Commitment is in respect of family, job, community etc. A sense of control over events is also healthy as it enables the hardy person to feel he or she is effective and able to control life outcomes.

Kobasa's research with 670 senior executives showed that those with high hardiness and high stress experienced less illness than those with low hardiness and high stress. This supports the view that hardiness is a key factor in combating stress.

One problem with hardiness is that it may be a factor that occurs more in men than in women and therefore may mediate the effects of stress differently for males and females. In addition, hardiness may not protect a person long term, as Rowe (1997) showed that even hardy people suffer from burn out in jobs like social work.

Neither is the relationship between control and stress straightforward. Rotter's work on locus of control showed how a balance of internal and external locus is most beneficial. It allows people to feel they have some control, but not to be so bound by control that they become distressed about things they cannot have any control over.

Another factor that mediates stress is personality type. Friedman and Rosenman found that people with a type A personality (competitive, self-critical, time urgent, angry and hostile) are more likely to suffer adverse effects of stress, particularly CHD, than type B personalities who show broadly the opposite traits. In their study two groups of men, type As and type Bs, were compared. The type A men worked longer hours and had a family history of heart disease. They showed how personality type was probably inherited and was linked to cardiovascular problems. Type As have since been found to show higher blood pressure, heart rate and stress hormone levels in response to stress. Recently, a type C has been identified: a passive, emotionally suppressant person who deals with stress by denial (Holland and Lewis). This type has been related to risk of developing depression and cancer. Although the idea of types A, B and C are generally accepted, it is now thought that hostility may be the key factor in response to stress.

One problem with all of the personal variables mentioned is that they are usually assessed using self-report measures which are not objective and therefore not scientific. In the case of personality type, however, behavioural measures are also taken, which allows researchers to cross-check the two measures for reliability.

This is an excellent answer. The candidate gains all 4 description marks for accurate and detailed description of hardiness and personality types. There is also description of two studies, which could have gained knowledge marks if there had not been sufficient material for full marks elsewhere. In the first paragraph, AO2 credit is awarded for explanation of how two of the elements of hardiness mediate the effects of stress. In the second paragraph, 3 AO2 marks are awarded for use of evidence to support assertions about the role of hardiness and the analytical points about gender and long-term effects. In the third paragraph, there is creditworthy analysis of the complex interaction between levels of perceived control and stress. In the fourth paragraph, 3 AO2 marks are awarded for analysis of how stress affects both type A and type C personalities and for the point about hostility being more important than general type. The final paragraph gains a further 2 AO2 marks for discussion of the underpinning methods. This response easily fits the descriptor for the excellent band and definitely deserves full marks for this section (AO1 = 4, AO2 = 8).

Total for this question: 20 out of 20 marks

Applied options

Substance abuse

(a) (i) Describe how a youth worker might use social inoculation with
teenagers as a way preventing solvent abuse. (4 marks)

(ii) Explain *one* strength and *one* limitation of social inoculation as a way
of preventing substance abuse. (4 marks)

(b) Discuss hereditary factors as an explanation for substance abuse. Refer to
evidence in your answer. (12 marks)

Total: 20 marks

(a) Part (i) assesses your knowledge of social inoculation for preventing substance abuse
and your ability to transfer that knowledge to an applied situation. Start by outlining
social inoculation in general and then explain how it might be used with teenagers
at risk of solvent abuse. It is important in these applied scenario questions to make
your idea for application as concrete as possible. In part (ii), you get 1 mark each for
giving a relevant strength and limitation and a further mark each for elaboration
(extended explanation saying how or why it constitutes a strength or limitation, or
an example that illustrates the nature of the strength or limitation).

(b) You need to describe hereditary factors and associated evidence for 4 marks, with
a further 8 marks for discussion. This might include the use of evidence to support
points, evaluation of the importance of hereditary factors and discussion of
possible alternatives — note these must be presented in the context of the
discussion to gain credit. Remember that unless you give evidence, you will gain a
maximum of 8 marks.

■ ■ ■

Answer to question 7: candidate A

(a) (i) Social inoculation is where people have an inoculation process so that they
can avoid solvent abuse if ever they are in a tricky situation. This might involve
role plays and maybe modelling someone else, like a youth worker, who says
'No!' with strong assertive body language. Another important part of inoculation is group discussion about consequences.

✎ The first sentence is not worthy of any credit. 2 marks are awarded for the second
sentence, which gives a relevant aspect of the process and elaborates with an
example. A further mark is given for another aspect of social inoculation in the final
sentence, but there is no applied example. A total of 3 marks are given.

(ii) A strength is that it works well. It is better to inoculate people before they begin to abuse than to try to make them give up once they have started. An abuser can easily end up being physically dependent, which is harder to deal with. A limitation is the cost. It would be expensive to have to do this with everyone at risk of substance abuse and where would the money come from?

> Saying that a treatment or therapy 'works well' without any evidence to back up the statement is not worthy of credit. The second point about prevention rather than cure is valid and well elaborated, for 2 marks. The point about cost is a tricky one. Examiners rarely credit cost as an answer unless there is some attempt to quantify the costs or to compare the costs. No marks are awarded for the limitation.

(b) Inheritance means whether something is genetic, passed on in DNA from parent to child, in this case substance abuse. Studies have been done with parents and children to see if they are both abusers. This happens as has been found by Peters and Preedy, who showed 18% of alcohol abusers who were adopted had real parents with alcohol problems as well. This was not as much in the control group. Twin studies also show higher concordance rates in MZ twins than in DZ twins.

Another cause of substance abuse could be personality, as extroverts were shown by Flory to be more likely to be substance abusers. This could be because they are always looking for excitement because their nervous systems are naturally low in arousal and they want more arousal.

Psychodynamic psychologists believe that substance abuse is not genetic, but that it is due to upbringing. If children's needs are not met when they are little, they grow up to be always looking for comfort, and drugs and alcohol are a way of getting that substitute comfort. This cannot be inheritance then but instead must be a result of experience and how people are treated. Also, just because identical twins are similar for alcohol abuse that does not mean that the behaviour is inherited. Twins often grow up together and so they are treated more similarly, especially identical ones.

> The candidate has missed several opportunities for gaining marks. Ideas are not always fully developed or not sufficiently linked to the question. Credit is given for basic knowledge of hereditary factors in the first sentence. The reasonable description of the Peters and Preedy study earns another AO1 mark. It is a shame that the candidate did not explain how this evidence supports the role of hereditary factors to gain an AO2 mark as well. The sentence about twin studies is too general. The next paragraph about personality factors is irrelevant to the question. In the final paragraph, the candidate appears to be making the same mistake again, as the first two sentences simply describe a possible alternative explanation. However, towards the middle of the paragraph, the candidate sets the alternative explanation against the role of hereditary factors, for 1 evaluation mark. A further evaluation mark is awarded for the discussion of problems with twin studies. In all, this is a weak average-to-poor band answer (AO1 = 2, AO2 = 2).

Total for this question: 9 out of 20 marks

Answer to question 7: candidate B

(a) (i) Social inoculation is giving people what they need to resist peer pressure to abuse. It normally involves four aspects: giving knowledge, discussion, skill development and public commitment. In this case, you could get an expert to come to talk to the teenagers about the effects of solvents on the body. You could get mums of former solvent sniffers to join in a discussion about how the family is affected. In a role play they could practise saying 'No' if ever a 'friend' asks them to join in with solvent abuse. Finally, they could make 'No to solvents' wristbands and wear them every day for a week.

> *This detailed answer gets full marks. The ideas for application are concrete, fully developed and relevant to the context. In fact, just two of these ideas would suffice for full marks.*

(ii) One strength is that it has been found to be effective in the long term. McAllister showed how teenagers treated with social inoculation for smoking were much less likely to have taken up smoking even years later. A problem is that those delivering the programme should be similar to the target group or a high status celebrity for it to be effective. This means programmes delivered by ordinary youth workers may not be useful or influential.

> *Both strength and limitation are valid and appropriately elaborated. Note how the candidate answers explicitly, making it clear which is the strength and which is the limitation. This answer is awarded the full 4 marks.*

(b) Some types of substance abuse may be inherited, but most research in this area has focused on alcohol. Melo's experiments showed it was possible to selectively breed for a preference for alcohol, so preference for alcohol must be genetic.

Kaij (1960) investigated concordance rates for alcohol abuse in identical and non-identical twins and found a rate of 54% in identicals who share 100% of their genetic material. In comparison, for non-identicals who only share 50% of genes, the rate was 28%. The higher rate for twins who share more of their genes strongly indicates a genetic component. However, the concordance rate for identical twins is not 100% and therefore there must also be some environmental influence. Indeed, higher rates in identical pairs are just what environmentalists would expect due to the more shared environment of identical pairs. There are also problems with twin evidence as samples tend to be small.

Adoption studies compare the behaviour of adopted children with that of their biological parents. Goldstein (1994) found that alcohol abusers who were adopted were much more likely to have biological parents with an alcohol abuse problem.

Gene mapping techniques have linked a specific dopamine receptor gene to alcohol and cocaine abuse, supporting the role of inheritance in substance abuse. As previously noted, most evidence relates to alcohol use and there is little evidence in relation to other substances.

The usual position in relation to the effect of genetics on behaviour is that genes pre-dispose an individual, but the development of the condition may be triggered by factors such as stress. Maybe people have the gene for substance abuse but do not always develop it because they do not experience the necessary trigger events. Plomin's view is different. He argues that alcohol abusers have genes that create an absence of brakes effect for control of alcohol intake, so people with this gene are unable to recognise when they should stop drinking.

The role of inheritance in substance abuse may be complex. If personality types are largely inherited and some personality types, particularly antisocial, play a significant role in alcohol abuse, abusing may be inherited indirectly. Morgenstern (1997) identified personality traits and patterns of alcohol abuse in 336 partici-pants and concluded that APD is significantly associated with alcohol abuse.

A different approach to abusing is taken by those who believe that peer pressure and modelling affect whether or not someone abuses substances. Maybe genetic pre-disposition is a factor, but perhaps only those who are exposed to social pressure and inappropriate models develop substance abuse in the end. Alternatively, perhaps people first use a substance because of social pressures, but only those with genes for abuse go on to develop full-blown abuse.

This is an excellent top-band answer. The candidate gains maximum AO1 credit for fully describing how inheritance may be involved in substance abuse. Evaluation, analysis and use of evidence are spread liberally throughout the answer. In the first paragraph, the candidate explains the relevance of evidence from selective breeding experiments, gaining an AO2 mark. More credit is awarded where evidence from twin studies is used effectively. A further 2 AO2 marks are awarded for the discussion/evaluation of how twin study evidence should be interpreted and the reference to small samples. The brief comment about research being largely restricted to alcohol abuse is just about worthy of credit as analysis. The discussion about the interaction between genes and environment is given AO2 credit. The clever analysis of the possible indirect inheritance of alcohol abuse via inherited personality is also awarded AO2 credit. In the final paragraph, a further 2 AO2 marks are awarded for the alternative explanation and for discussion of how inheritance and social factors might interact. Maximum marks are awarded (AO1 = 4, AO2 = 8).

Total for this question: 20 out of 20 marks

Applied options

Forensic psychology

(a) **Outline and briefly evaluate *one* alternative to official statistics as a way of measuring crime.** (4 marks)

(b) **A prison governor decides to set up a behaviour modification system in his prison. Explain what is meant by *behaviour modification* and how it might be used to treat offenders in a prison.** (4 marks)

(c) **Many politicians argue that prison does not work and suggest that there are other, better alternatives. Discuss the effectiveness of custodial sentencing in the treatment of offenders. Refer to evidence in your answer.** (12 marks)

Total: 20 marks

(a) Here, 2 marks are available for knowledge/description of an alternative to official statistics and 2 marks are for a brief evaluation. These 2 marks can be gained by mentioning two evaluative points briefly or for expanding on one.

(b) In this section, 2 marks are to be gained by showing knowledge of what is meant by behaviour modification. This means you should give a brief description. Make sure you include the most important aspects of behaviour modification. The other 2 marks are for application of that knowledge to a prison situation. Make your ideas as concrete as possible and try to imagine exactly what would be possible in a prison. For example, using sweets as reinforcement might be appropriate if using behaviour modification in a primary school but not in a prison. In this sort of application question, less able candidates often simply repeat the general description, adding words such as 'in prison' to try and make the answer applied. You need to make your suggestion practical and express it in concrete terms by saying exactly what would happen.

(c) Start this part by outlining the role or aims of custodial sentencing. This is really describing what prison is for and would be an easy way to get description marks. Description marks could also be awarded for knowledge of studies or factual information, for example recidivism rates. Having outlined the aims, you can then go on to determine whether or not these aims are being met and, if so, how effectively this is being done. For discussion, it is important to discuss recidivism, as one of the key aims of prison is generally thought to be reform. You might also refer to any negative consequences of custodial sentencing as part of your answer. The first sentence of the question mentions 'better alternatives', which seems to be inviting you to make comparisons. Use of evidence and evaluation of evidence is another way to gain discussion marks here. Remember to include at least a brief reference to evidence – this might just be the findings of a study – otherwise the marks would be limited to 8 for this section.

Answer to question 8: candidate A

(a) Victim surveys involve asking people whether or not they have been a victim of crime. This is compared to official statistics, which only include crimes that have been reported and recorded and there are lots of reasons why some crimes are not reported or recorded. So there is a 'dark figure' of crime that official statistics do not include.

> ✍ This answer gets only 1 mark. Although the candidate starts with a brief outline of a valid alternative way of measuring crime, the answer then strays into a discussion of official statistics. The candidate should have given a little more description of victim surveys as a method and then made some direct evaluation. It would have been easy to say how victim surveys help to reveal the 'dark figure' of crime. This candidate clearly knows the relevant information but seems to have forgotten the question.

(b) Behaviour modification is really operant conditioning so prisoners could get given tokens for being good. They could then exchange the tokens for other things — treats that they might want like cigarettes and watching videos etc. This would then make their good behaviour more likely in the future.

> ✍ 1 mark is awarded for knowledge of behaviour modification. The candidate says that it is based on operant conditioning and that it (use of reinforcement) makes good behaviour more likely to occur in the future. If positive reinforcement had been explicitly mentioned, the description would have been complete. The application to a prison environment is only half done. There is a description of the type of privileges to be earned, but the candidate has not specified the desired behaviour sufficiently. 1 mark is awarded for application, giving 2 marks for this section as a whole.

(c) Prison can have disastrous consequences. People often cannot get jobs once they get out and are unable to look after themselves. They might offend again deliberately to get back into prison where they feel comfortable and do not have to make decisions.

Re-offending rates are high (70%) and this could be because prison is a school for crime. When a young person happens to end up in prison, he or she might be in a cell with a more hardened and experienced criminal and therefore learn his criminal ways. This means that re-offending will be high because they have learnt to be a worse criminal. This means custodial sentences are not effective, but at least they keep people off the streets so the public are safe. This is called incapacitation.

One study showed that prison officers can be dehumanising to the prisoners and this can make them stressed and mentally ill, which means they are not being improved by prison, but the opposite.

So what else can be done to deal with offenders? A system that is quite new is restorative justice. This means that offenders have to make amends to their victim or to society. This is better than prison because then at least the person must confront the consequences of their offence and this could lead to real regret, whereas prison might just make them more resentful of the system and just make them harder.

The first paragraph touches on several negative effects of custodial sentencing, although these are all expressed in rather anecdotal terms. Had the candidate referred to institutionalisation, prisonisation or brutalisation, this might have been a more persuasive paragraph. In its present form, this paragraph as a whole is awarded 1 AO2 mark for analysis of the problems associated with custodial sentencing. In the second paragraph, 2 AO1 marks are awarded for the knowledge of recidivism rates (admittedly this is rather vague, but 70% is approximately the figure in studies of young males) and for the point about incapacitation. An evaluation mark is also awarded in this paragraph for the further elaboration of brutalisation. The point about the effects of prison on mental health is worthy of 1 AO2 mark, but there is insufficient description of the study, presumably Zimbardo, for AO1 credit. The final paragraph neatly compares prison with an alternative — restorative justice — and explains how the latter may offer a better solution. This is quite well expressed and worthy of 2 AO2 marks. There is no real evidence here except for the brief reference to recidivism rates and Zimbardo, neither of which are covered in any detail. Had this candidate accrued more than 8 marks overall, it is likely that the examiner would have reduced the mark to 8 because the answer lacks evidence (AO1 = 2, AO2 = 5).

Total for this question: 10 out of 20 marks

■ ■ ■

Answer to question 8: candidate B

(a) One alternative is offender self-reporting. This is where offenders tell interviewers what other crimes they have committed. Alternatively, it might be a group of likely offenders, such as young males, and they are asked about what crimes they have committed. The trouble with this is that people might exaggerate to make it seem like they are tough, so the results may not be a reliable, objective measure of crimes committed.

This answer includes a useful outline of the way of measuring crime and a brief but sensible evaluative point that is expressed using specialist terminology. This response scores the full 4 marks.

(b) Behaviour modification is a behaviourist technique for behaviour change, which uses operant conditioning principles identified by Skinner and is based on reinforcement (reward). Use of positive reinforcement helps to encourage good behaviour in the future. Prisoners could be given tokens (token economy) for working in the prison kitchen and attending classes. These tokens could then be used to buy privileges like phone calls home and extra visits from family.

Behaviour modification is clearly described using appropriate psychological terminology. The application to a prison setting is fully appropriate; the candidate describes both the desired behaviour and the type of reward to be earned with the tokens in objective terms. This answer deserves the full 4 marks.

(c) Custodial sentencing is thought to have four aims. The first is reform, meaning that prison should make the offender a better person in the future. It could be argued that prison does not meet this aim as many people who go into prison re-offend within 2 years of release (Cullen and Minchin, 2000). This figure is especially high for young males, 76% of whom re-offend. This suggests that the second aim of deterrence is not being met either. Deterrence means to put people off offending. Certainly the many who re-offend are not deterred by the prospect of another prison sentence.

The third aim of prison is incapacitation – the offender is prevented from carrying out further offences while serving a sentence. This aim is met in as much as the public is safe for the duration of the offender's sentence, but as most sentences are short and many prisoners are released early due to over-crowding, even this aim is not ideally met.

The final aim of custodial sentencing is retribution. This means society getting its own back and making the offender pay. Davis and Raymond, in their judicial review, suggested that retribution is the main purpose served by prison sentences. However, perhaps there are better ways to make offenders pay back to society. They could make good what they did by apologising to the victim and even paying them back in real terms or financially. This brings victim and offender face to face and may result in true remorse as the offender empathises with their victim and sees the consequences of his or her crime, something that prison does not do. Systems of restorative justice bring offenders and victims together in this way for psychological healing. Sherman and Strang (2007) compared restorative justice and conventional programmes and found that it reduced recidivism and benefited victims who had less desire for revenge and lower stress levels.

The overall effectiveness of custodial sentencing probably depends on whether the offender gets any treatment while in prison. If prisoners can attend classes like anger management that can help them to understand their behaviour and maybe change it in the future, then prison would be worthwhile. Sadly, prisons are overcrowded (population is currently over 80,000) and resources are stretched, so many prisoners do not get any treatment or education when they are inside.

In this case, it might be better to keep them out of prison but under some form of supervision, like probation. A recent idea is ankle tagging. This makes sure offenders keep a night curfew, incapacitating them from further offending in a similar way to prison. Cassidy (2005) found tagging was effective in preventing breach of conditions imposed by the court, decreasing breaches by 7%. However, unlike when in prison, offenders can maintain family relationships, hopefully helping them to keep out of trouble in the future and preventing them from being hardened by prison experiences. In conclusion, prison does not seem to meet the aims and perhaps there are other alternatives that are just as effective, if not more so.

This is an excellent answer. The candidate shows ample knowledge for the full 4 marks. There is a clear outline of the four aims of custodial sentencing and

8

question

evidence in relation to recidivism rates, restorative justice and tagging. There is also some description of alternatives. The discussion is wide-ranging and appears throughout the answer. In the first paragraph, 2 discussion marks are awarded for explanations of how prison neither reforms nor deters. In the second paragraph, the candidate explores the issue of incapacitation and gains another discussion mark. The third paragraph is a highly effective comparison of prison and restorative justice, which gains a total of 3 discussion marks. In the fourth paragraph, the candidate makes the point that prison could be positive but rarely is because so many prisoners get no treatment or education. This discussion of possibilities for improvements while in prison gains 2 further marks. Note how this leads neatly on to the next paragraph, where the candidate talks about another alternative and again compares it effectively with prison. This discussion of tagging as an alternative gains a further 2 marks; tagging is linked to incapacitation and the candidate explains how keeping the offender out of prison might prevent the negative effects of custodial sentencing. In all, this answer is a well-structured and clearly argued response worthy of a top-band mark (AO1 = 4, AO2 = 8).

Total for this question: 20 out of 20 marks